T0347890

# Security, Privacy, and Anonymization in Social Networks:

## Emerging Research and Opportunities

B. K. Tripathy
*VIT University, India*

Kiran Baktha
*VIT University, India*

A volume in the Advances in
Information Security, Privacy, and
Ethics (AISPE) Book Series

Published in the United States of America by
    IGI Global
    Information Science Reference (an imprint of IGI Global)
    701 E. Chocolate Avenue
    Hershey PA, USA 17033
    Tel: 717-533-8845
    Fax: 717-533-8661
    E-mail: cust@igi-global.com
    Web site: http://www.igi-global.com

Library of Congress Cataloging-in-Publication Data

Names: Tripathy, B. K., 1957- author. | Baktha, Kiran, 1995- author.
Title: Security, privacy, and anonymization in social networks : emerging
  research and opportunities / by B.K. Tripathy and Kiran Baktha.
Description: Hershey, PA : Information Science Reference, [2018]
Identifiers: LCCN 2017036591| ISBN 9781522551584 (hardcover) | ISBN
  9781522551591 (ebook)
Subjects: LCSH: Online social networks--Security measures. | Computer
  crimes--Prevention. | Privacy, Right of. | Anonymous persons. |
  Confidential communications.
Classification: LCC TK5105.59 .T75 2018 | DDC 006.7/54--dc23 LC record available at https://
lccn.loc.gov/2017036591

This book is published in the IGI Global book series Advances in Information Security, Privacy, and Ethics (AISPE) (ISSN: 1948-9730; eISSN: 1948-9749)

British Cataloguing in Publication Data
A Cataloguing in Publication record for this book is available from the British Library.

All work contributed to this book is new, previously-unpublished material.
The views expressed in this book are those of the authors, but not necessarily of the publisher.

For electronic access to this publication, please contact: eresources@igi-global.com.

# Advances in Information Security, Privacy, and Ethics (AISPE) Book Series

ISSN:1948-9730
EISSN:1948-9749

Editor-in-Chief: Manish Gupta, State University of New York, USA

## MISSION

As digital technologies become more pervasive in everyday life and the Internet is utilized in ever increasing ways by both private and public entities, concern over digital threats becomes more prevalent.

The **Advances in Information Security, Privacy, & Ethics (AISPE) Book Series** provides cutting-edge research on the protection and misuse of information and technology across various industries and settings. Comprised of scholarly research on topics such as identity management, cryptography, system security, authentication, and data protection, this book series is ideal for reference by IT professionals, academicians, and upper-level students.

## COVERAGE

- Security Information Management
- IT Risk
- Cookies
- Technoethics
- Network Security Services
- Privacy-Enhancing Technologies
- Cyberethics
- Risk Management
- Data Storage of Minors
- CIA Triad of Information Security

IGI Global is currently accepting manuscripts for publication within this series. To submit a proposal for a volume in this series, please contact our Acquisition Editors at Acquisitions@igi-global.com or visit: http://www.igi-global.com/publish/.

# Titles in this Series

*For a list of additional titles in this series, please visit:*
*https://www.igi-global.com/book-series/advances-information-security-privacy-ethics/37157*

**The Morality of Weapons Design and Development Emerging Research and Opportunities**
John Forge (University of Sydney, Australia)
Information Science Reference • ©2018 • 216pp • H/C (ISBN: 9781522539841) • US $175.00

**Advanced Cloud Computing Security Techniques and Applications**
Ihssan Alkadi (Independent Researcher, USA)
Information Science Reference • ©2018 • 350pp • H/C (ISBN: 9781522525066) • US $225.00

**Algorithmic Strategies for Solving Complex Problems in Cryptography**
Kannan Balasubramanian (Mepco Schlenk Engineering College, India) and M. Rajakani (Mepco Schlenk Engineering College, India)
Information Science Reference • ©2018 • 302pp • H/C (ISBN: 9781522529156) • US $245.00

**Information Technology Risk Management and Compliance in Modern Organizations**
Manish Gupta (State University of New York, Buffalo, USA) Raj Sharman (State University of New York, Buffalo, USA) John Walp (M&T Bank Corporation, USA) and Pavankumar Mulgund (State University of New York, Buffalo, USA)
Business Science Reference • ©2018 • 360pp • H/C (ISBN: 9781522526049) • US $225.00

**Detecting and Mitigating Robotic Cyber Security Risks**
Raghavendra Kumar (LNCT Group of College, India) Prasant Kumar Pattnaik (KIIT University, India) and Priyanka Pandey (LNCT Group of College, India)
Information Science Reference • ©2017 • 384pp • H/C (ISBN: 9781522521549) • US $210.00

**Advanced Image-Based Spam Detection and Filtering Techniques**
Sunita Vikrant Dhavale (Defense Institute of Advanced Technology (DIAT), Pune, India)
Information Science Reference • ©2017 • 213pp • H/C (ISBN: 9781683180135) • US $175.00

*For an entire list of titles in this series, please visit:*
*https://www.igi-global.com/book-series/advances-information-security-privacy-ethics/37157*

701 East Chocolate Avenue, Hershey, PA 17033, USA
Tel: 717-533-8845 x100 • Fax: 717-533-8661
E-Mail: cust@igi-global.com • www.igi-global.com

# Table of Contents

# Preface

## INTRODUCTION

A social network consists of a finite set or sets of actors (Social entities, which can be discrete individual, corporate, or collective social units) and the relation (a collection of the defining feature that establishes a linkage between a pair of actors) or relations defined on them. The social networks, as they disseminate massive amounts of personal data on individual behaviour, probably lead to the erosion of civil liberties through loss of privacy and personal freedom. Social network analysis is concerned with uncovering patterns in the connection between entities. The network analyst would seek to model these relationships to depict the structure of the group. Social networks contain valuable information about the society and publishing them tends to provide information for data analysers or scientists. The publication of data for such studies through analysis, may lead to disclosure of sensitive information of the respondents. However, withholding data because of the privacy concerns would make analysis impossible and one cannot derive useful information. So, some steps are needed to be taken before the publication of social network data such that their publication will not disclose the sensitive information of the respondents easily. The process of deriving a social network from the original one such that there will be very little threat for disclosure of sensitive information disclosure is termed as privacy protection /preservation.

Recent years have seen exceptional growth in the usage of online social networks and there are more than 300 online social networks. Users can upload pictures of themselves to their profiles, post blog entries for others to read, search for other users with similar interests and compile and share lists of contacts. The information they share are not only viewed by the trusted users but also by the adversaries. Over the years several techniques have been developed to secure user information in social networks. There are several edited volumes where articles have been published from different angles. One of the most popular approaches in this direction is anonymization of the social networks before publication. Again we find multiple approaches for social network anonymization. We have provided an exhaustive and comparative description of these techniques in a single place by describing an exclusive coverage of various anonymization techniques developed for social networks. These techniques have a permanent problem of information loss and every effort is made to have minimum information loss in this process.

## ORGANIZATION OF THE BOOK

The first chapter provides basic concepts related to social networks, including their representation techniques. In Chapter 2 emphases is given on anonymisation techniques. In Chapter 3, we focus on a specific attack on privacy of social networks, called the neighbourhood attack and provide anonymisation algorithms which can handle it. A popular approach to anonymise social networks is the clustering approach. We discuss the different algorithms developed for anonymisation of social networks so far, in this chapter. In Chapter 5 we discuss the other important approach for social network anonymisation, the graph modification approach and the various algorithms developed following this approach. Weighted and directed graphs are two special types of graphs, which are often used to represent social networks. We discuss the anonymisation techniques for such graphs in Chapter 6. A related problem is the process of de-anonymization, through which interpretation of results after analysis can be made with respect to original data. We discuss on the de-anonymisation of anonymised social networks in Chapter 7. It is interesting to note that the de-anonymisation techniques are very certain and most of the authors claim that complete de-anonymisation of all kinds of anonymised social networks are possible. Even, some of them have suggested that their de-anonymisation techniques can be used to verify the efficiency of the anonymisation algorithms. Case studies have been included in most of the chapters for clear understanding of the concepts and techniques. The trends of research in different directions of anonymization of social networks are to be critically analyzed with problems for continuing further research and their current status are to be presented. We have provided bibliography of papers consulted during the compilation of this piece of work at the end of every chapter.

We have selected some of the trends on the topic and also stated some other similar techniques briefly in this monograph keeping the length of the monograph in view. It is our belief that this monograph will solve the purpose of a go to source for researchers, practitioners and post-graduate students on the topic.

*B. K. Tripathy*
*VIT University, India*

*Kiran Baktha*
*VIT University, India*

# Chapter 1
# Fundamentals of Social Networks

## ABSTRACT

*A social network is comprised of a finite set of actors, who are social entities. These entities can be discrete individuals, corporate, or collective social units. They are related to each other through some relations, establishing some linkage among them. Social networks have grown in popularity as they enable researchers to study not only social actors but their social relationships. Moreover, many important aspects of societal networks and their study lead to the study of behavioural science. The scientific study of network data can reveal important behaviour of the elements involved and social trends. It also provides insight for suitable changes in the social structure and roles of individuals in it. Important aspects of societal life are organised as networks. The importance of networks in society has put social network analysis at the forefront of social and behavioural science research. The presence of relational information is a critical and defining feature of a social network. This chapter explores social networks.*

## INTRODUCTION

A social network comprises of a finite set of actors, who are social entities. These entities can be discrete individuals, corporate or collective social units. They are related to each other through some relations, establishing some linkage among them. Social network has grown in popularity as it enables

DOI: 10.4018/978-1-5225-5158-4.ch001

researchers to study not only social actors but their social relationships. Moreover, many important aspects of societal networks and their study lead to the study of behavioural science. Scientific study of network data can reveal much important behaviour of the elements involved and social trends. It also provides insight for suitable changes in the social structure and roles of individuals in it. Important aspects of societal life are organised as networks. The importance of networks in society has put social network analysis at the forefront of social and behavioural science research. The presence of relational information is a critical and defining feature of a social network. Social network analysis is concerned with uncovering patterns in the connections between entities. It has been widely applied to organisational networks to classify the influence or popularity of individuals and to detect collusion and fraud. Social network analysis can also be applied to study disease transmission in communities, the functioning of computer networks and emergent behaviour of physical and biological systems. The network analyst would seek to model these relationships to depict the structure of a group. One can then study the impact of this structure on the functioning of the group and /or the influence of this structure on individuals within the group. The social network perspective thus has a distinctive orientation in which structures may be behavioural, social, political, or economic.

The advent of social network sites in the last few years seems to be a trend that will likely continue in the years to come. This has accelerated the research in the field. Online social interaction has become very popular around the globe and most sociologists agree that this will not fade away. Such a development has been possible due to the advancements in computer power, technologies and the spread of the World Wide Web.

## SOCIAL NETWORK ANALYSIS

Scientific study of social network data can reveal many important behaviours of the elements involved and social trends and provides insight for suitable changes in the social structure and roles of individuals in it. There are many evidences which indicate the precious value of social network analysis in shedding light on social behaviour, health and well- being of the general public. Social network analysis provides a formal, conceptual means for thinking about the social world. Freeman has argued that the methods of social network analysis provide formal statements about social properties and processes. Social network analysis thus allows a flexible set of concepts and methods with broad interdisciplinary appeal. It provides a formal, conceptual means for thinking about the social world. It is based on an assumption of the importance of relationships among interacting units. Of critical importance for the development of methods for social network analysis is the fact that the unit of analysis in network analysis is not the individual but an entity consisting of a collection of individuals, each of whom in turn is tied to a few, some or many others, and so on. It attempts to solve analytical problems that are nonstandard. The data are analyzed using social network methods and are quite different from the data typically encountered in social methods encountered in social and behavioural sciences. However, social network analysis is explicitly interested in the interrelatedness of social units. The dependencies among the units are measured with structural variables. Theories that incorporate network ideas are distinguished by propositions about the relations among social units. Such theories argue that units are not acting independently from one another but rather influence each other. Focusing on such structural variables opens up a different range of possibilities for and constraints on data analysis and model building. Instead of analyzing individual behaviours, attitudes and beliefs, social network analysis focuses its attention on social entities or actors in interaction with one another and on how these interactions constitute a framework or structure that can be studied and analysed in its own right (Wasserman & Faust, 1994).

The goal of social network analysis is to uncover hidden social patterns. The power of social network analysis has been shown much stronger than that of traditional methods which focus on analysing the attributes of individual social actors. In social network analysis, the relationships and ties between social actors in a network are often regarded more important and informative than the attributes of individual social actors. Social network analysis approaches have been shown very useful in capturing and explaining many real-world phenomena such as "small world phenomenon" (Wasserman & Faust, 1994).

## SOCIAL NETWORK REPRESENTATION

Two kinds of representation techniques using mathematical tools are followed for social networks; graphs and matrices. A social network consists of a set of actors that may have relationships with each other. The number of actors may be a few or can be large in number. The number of relations between a pair of actors can be of one or more kinds. For an efficient understanding of a social network, the understanding of the relationships and their patterns is

3

highly essential. One needs to know all the relationships that exist between each pair of actors in the population (Hanneman, 1998)..

Mathematical tools are used for representation in order to have a compact and systematic model, which is easy and efficient for analysis. One of the necessities is the use of computers to store and manipulate these models. It will provide good storage facilities and quick manipulation of information which are also accurate. Manual representation and manipulation ceases to be applicable as the size of the network increases in terms of more number of actors or high number of relations among them (Hanneman, 1998)..

Also, the representation through mathematical models may uncover some properties of the network, which we might have skipped while using words for representations (Hanneman, 1998).

## Graphical Representation of Social networks

Graphs are very useful mathematical models having many applications in Mathematics, Computer Science and other fields. Graphical representation of networks helps in visualisation of the networks, the actors and their relationships (Harary, 1960; Wassermann & Faust, 1994; Deo, 1974)

**Definition 1:** A graph G is a pair (V, E), where V is a set of vertices and E is a set of edges such that each edge connects a pair of vertices. The pair of vertices connected by a n edge is called its end vertices.

Unless otherwise specified, we will always assume our graphs are finite. A self-loop is an edge with the end vertices identical.

In a basic graph there is no ordering of the pair of end vertices. In the graphical representation of a social network, the actors or events are represented by vertices and their relationship or connections are represented by edges.

**Example 1:** In Figure 1, we have 6 vertices (A, B, C, D, E, F} and 7 edges {e1, e2, e3, e4, e5, e6, e7}. The edge e1 is connecting the vertices A and B. So, it has end vertices {e1, e2}.

**Definition 2:** A path in a undirected graph is an alternating sequence of vertices and edges, stating with a vertex and ending with another vertex. If the start and end vertices are identical the path is said to be closed otherwise it is said to be open.

In a directed graph, in addition to the above, the edges must be in the same direction. A graph is said to be simple if it has no self-loops.

Referring to Figure 1, a path between vertices A and F is $e1 \rightarrow e6 \rightarrow e7$.

A circuit is formed by the vertices B, D, E and F.

The distance is defined as the number of edges on the shortest path between the vertices.

The eccentricity ecc(v) of a vertex' v' in a graph G is the greatest distance from 'v' to any other node.

For example, in Figure 1 ecc(A) = 3.

The radius rad(G) of G is the value of the smallest eccentricity.

The radius of the graph in Figure 1 is 2.

The diameter diam(G) of G is the value of the greatest eccentricity.

The diameter of the graph in Figure 1 is 3.

The centre of G is the set of nodes v such that ecc(v) = rad(G)

In Figure 1, centre of G is {B, E}.

**Definition 3:** A graph is said to be connected if there is at least one path between every pair of vertices. Otherwise it is said to be disconnected. A circuit is a closed path.

The graph in Figure 1 is connected.

The graph in Figure 2 is disconnected as there is no path from any vertex to the vertex D. The vertex D has degree 0 and is called an isolated vertex.

*Figure 1. A basic graph*

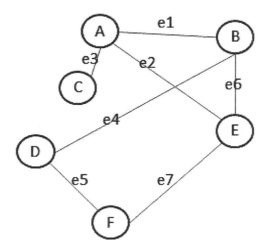

*Figure 2. A disconnected graph*

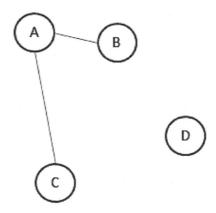

As there is the notion of directed graphs, basic graphs are also called as non-directional graphs/ undirected graphs. A directed graph is a graph, where the edges are directed in the sense that the associations are from one vertex to another. If the association is from both sides, we use two oppositely directed edges between the pair of vertices. The directed edges are represented by arcs with an arrow head towards the directed vertex. In this representation each directed edge is a ordered pair.

An edge e is an ordered pair of vertices (u, v), where the edge is directed towards v. u is called the start vertex and v is called the end vertex of e.

**Example 2:** Suppose there are 5 people in a locality and they have friend relations among themselves but not that each one is a friend of every other member. Let us denote the five members as {A, B, C, D, E}. If X considers Y as a friend then we put a directed edge from X to Y. We can have a possible representation of this social network in the form of the directed graph as in Figure 3.

Social networks are represented by a graph that consists of nodes representing actors and edges to represent relations. In the sociological context this representations is called a "sociogram". The actors do often have levels associated with them.

**Definition 4:** There may be graphs where the relation is +ve or −ve or absent. A graph with signed data uses a '+' sign on the arrow to indicate a +ve

*Figure 3. A directed graph*

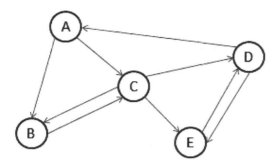

relationship, a '-' sign on the arrow to indicate a –ve relationship and no arrow to indicate neutral relationship. Such a graph is called signed directed graph or a signed digraph.

**Definition 5:** In a non-directional graph, the degree of a node is the number of edges meeting at that node. Each edge provides two degrees to a graph, one each to each of its end vertices.

In Figure 1, degree(A) = 3 and degree(C) = 1. Degree(F) = 2.

A node can be of even or odd degree. It can be observed that the sum of the degrees of all the vertices in a non-directional graph is always even. This observation leads to the fact that the number of odd vertices in a non-directional graph is always even.

In Figure 1, A is an odd vertex whereas F is an even vertex.

**Definition 6:** A tree is a connected graph without any circuits.

The graph in Figure 1 is not a tree as it has circuits. The graph in Figure 2 is not a tree as it is not connected.

**Definition 7:** A connected component (or just component) of an undirected graph is a subgraph in which any two vertices are connected to each other by paths, and which is connected to no additional vertices in the super graph.

A connected graph has only one component. In Figure 2 the subgraph formed by the vertices A, B, C is a component.

**Definition 8:** A subgraph of a undirected graph is said to be a spanning tree for the graph if it is a tree and passes through all the vertices of the graph.

In Figure 1, the subgraph formed with all the vertices in it and edges $\{e_1, e_3, e_5, e_6, e_7\}$ is a spanning tree.

**Definition 9:** A weighted graph is a graph which has weights attached to each of its edges. There is a weight function w: E→R, where R is the set of real numbers and w attaches a weight to each of the edges in the edge set E.

As an example, if we form a network of all cities in a country, then the weights may be the distance between the two cities.

In Figure 4, A, B, C, D represent cities and the numbers inscribed on the edges are the distance in Kilometre between the cities which they connect. So, the graph is a weighted graph.

**Definition 10:** A minimal spanning tree of a weighted graph is a spanning tree which has minimum weight, where the weight of a graph is the sum of the weights attached to all of its edges.

The weight of the graph in Figure 4 is 45.

*Figure 4. A weighted graph*

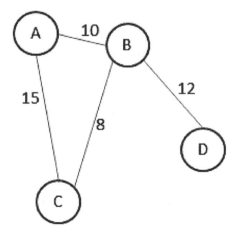

**Definition 11:** In a directed graph, a node is attached with two degrees. The number of edges directed towards it is called its "indegree" and the number of edges coming out of it is called its "outdegree".

For example, the indegree of vertex C in Figure 2 is '2' and the outdegree is also '2'.

**Definition 12:** A graph that represents a single kind of relation is called a simplex graph.

The graph in Figure 4, which represents cities and the distances between them, is a simplex graph.

However, many times social structures are multiplex, that is, there are multiple different kinds of ties among social actors. In such a graph, each kind of relation can be represented by a different colour for identification. Also, different line styles can also be used for the purpose (Figure 5).

**Definition 13:** Degree centrality is the most basic network measure and captures the number of ties to a given actor. For un-directed ties this is simply a count of the number of ties for every actor. For directed networks, actors can have both indegree and outdegree centrality scores.

*Figure 5. A multiplex graph*

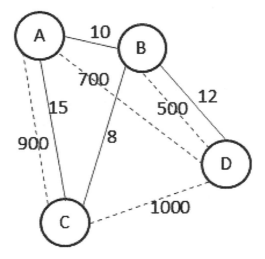

In Figure 4 the degree centralities of vertices A, B, C, D are 2, 3, 2, 1 respectively.

As the name implies, centrality measures how central or well-connected an actor is in a network. This theoretically signals importance or power and increased access to information or just general activity level and high degree centrality is generally considered to be an asset to an actor.

**Definition 14:** Betweenness Centrality is roughly defined as the number of shortest paths between alters that go through a particular actor. More precisely, it is the sum of the shortest path lengths between every set of alters where the path goes through the actor we are calculating the measure for divided by the shortest path lengths (not necessarily through the target actor) between those actors. This intuitively measures the degree to which information or relationships have to flow through a particular actor and their relative importance as an intermediary in the network.

In Figure 4, the Betweenness centrality of vertex A is 1 and that of C is 0.

**Definition 15:** Closeness centrality measures how many steps (ties) are required for a particular actor to access every other actor in the network. This is measured as 1 divided by the sum of geodesic distances from an actor to all alters in the network.

The measure will reach its maximum for a given network size when an actor is directly connected to all others in the network and its minimum when an actor is not connected to any others. This captures the intuition that short path lengths between actors signal that they are closer to each other. Note that this measure is sensitive to network size and is decreasing in the number of actors in the network. This makes intuitive sense in many situations because it gets more difficult to maintain close relationships with all members of the network as the network grows but can also be corrected for by multiplying by the number of actors in the network.

**Definition 16:** Eigenvector centrality measures the degree to which an actor is connected to other well connected actors. It takes advantage of a mathematical property of networks (represented as adjacency matrices) that allows for the easy calculation of how well connected an actor is to other well connected actors. While we will not get into the details of its calculation, this measure captures the value of having a lot of friends in high places.

The concept of Eigenvector centrality was introduced in Wassermann and Faust (1994), and Deo (1974). Consider A as an n × n adjacency matrix, then the eigenvector centrality $e_i$ of node i is defined as the i[th] entry of the normalized eigenvector corresponding to the largest Eigen value of A. Let, $\lambda$ be the largest Eigen value and x be the corresponding eigenvector, then,

$$Ax = \lambda x, \rightarrow x = \left(1 / \lambda\right) Ax \text{ and } x_i = \left(1 / \lambda\right) \sum a_{ij} x_j$$

## Matrix Representation of Graphs (Hanneman, 1998)

Graphs are very useful ways of representing information about a social network. For small size networks or with very few relationships it looks nice and easy to decipher. But, if the number of actors becomes reasonably large and/or the number of relationships becomes large, a graphical representation of a social network looks clumsy and becomes difficult for analysis.

An ideal solution to the above problem is to use the mathematical model of matrix to represent a social network.

**Definition 17:** A matrix is a rectangular array of elements arranged in horizontal rows and vertical columns. The dimension of a matrix having m rows and n columns is m x n.

$$A = \begin{bmatrix} 2 & 1 & 5 & 7 \\ 3 & 2 & 4 & 5 \\ 1 & 6 & 7 & -1 \end{bmatrix}$$

The above is a matrix of integers of dimension 3 x 4.

A matrix having the number of rows equal to the number of columns is called a square matrix. A matrix A is represented as $\left(a_{ij}\right)_{m \times n}$, where $a_{ij}$ represents the element in the ith row and jth column of the matrix and its dimension is m x n.

In the above matrix A is not a square matrix.

**Definition 18:** We can add two matrices only if both the matrices have the same dimension. Suppose $A = (a_{ij})_{m \times n}$ and $B = (b_{ij})_{m \times n}$ be two matrices. Then their sum C = A + B is a matrix of the same dimension m x n such that $c_{ij} = a_{ij} + b_{ij}, 1 \le i \le m; 1 \le j \le n$. Similarly, we can define D = A – B.

**Definition 19:** The transpose of a matrix A of dimension m x n is represented by $A^T$ is of dimension n x m such that $A^T = (a_{ji})$. Basically, $A^T$ is obtained from A by changing rows into columns and columns into rows.

**Definition 20:** A square matrix is said to be symmetric if and only if $A = A^T$. So, a square matrix is symmetric iff $a_{ij} = a_{ji}, 1 \le i, j \le n$. On the other hand A is said to be skew symmetric iff $A = -A^T$, i.e. $a_{ij} = -a_{ji}, 1 \le i, j \le n$.

The most common approach to represent a social network is using the adjacency matrix. Next, we define the notion of adjacency matrix.

**Definition 21:** The adjacency matrix of a non-directional graph G = (V, E) is a symmetric square matrix of dimension n x n, where |V| = n (cardinality of the vertex set V is n) such that if there is an edge between the ith and the jth node of G then $a_{ij} = a_{ji} = 1$; else $a_{ij} = a_{ji} = 0$.

As an example the adjacency matrix for the graph in Figure 1 is given by Table 1.

This adjacency matrix is symmetric. The number of 1s in the matrix is twice the number of edges. In case of sociograms the diagonal elements are sometimes ignored and are left blank.

*Table 1. The adjacency matrix of the graph in Figure 1*

|   | A | B | C | D | E | F |
|---|---|---|---|---|---|---|
| A | 0 | 1 | 1 | 0 | 1 | 0 |
| B | 1 | 0 | 0 | 1 | 1 | 0 |
| C | 1 | 0 | 0 | 0 | 0 | 0 |
| D | 0 | 1 | 0 | 0 | 0 | 1 |
| E | 1 | 1 | 0 | 0 | 0 | 1 |
| F | 0 | 0 | 0 | 1 | 1 | 0 |

*Table 2. The adjacency matrix of the graph in Figure 3*

|   | A | B | C | D | E |
|---|---|---|---|---|---|
| **A** | 0 | 1 | 1 | 0 | 0 |
| **B** | 0 | 0 | 1 | 0 | 0 |
| **C** | 0 | 1 | 0 | 1 | 1 |
| **D** | 1 | 0 | 0 | 0 | 1 |
| **E** | 0 | 0 | 0 | 1 | 0 |

This matrix is not symmetric. The number of 1s is equal to the number of directed edges in the graph.

If we transpose the adjacency matrix of a directed graph then the degree of similarity between an adjacency matrix and the transpose matrix is one way of summarizing the degree of symmetry in the pattern of relations among actors. To express it otherwise, the correlation between the adjacency matrix and its transpose is a measure of the degree of reciprocity of ties.

**Definition 22:** By matrix permutation, we mean simply changing the rows and columns of a matrix. Since the adjacency matrix of a unordered graph is symmetric, if the position of a row is changed then the position of the corresponding column must be changed.

**Definition 23:** Blocks of a matrix are formed by passing dividing lines through the matrix rows and columns. Passing the dividing lines is called partitioning the matrix. Partitioning is also called blocking the matrix as by partitioning a matrix blocks are formed.

## Adjacency Lists

There is a third common way to represent graphs, and this is with adjacency lists. Fix a (directed or undirected, simple or not) graph G = (V, E). We do not need to assume V is ordered or consists of numbers. An adjacency list for G is merely a list of all the vertices $v \in V$ together with its set of neighbours n(v)$\subset$ V ; where n(v) denotes the set of neighbours of 'v'. A vertex is said to be a neighbour of another vertex 'v' if it is connected to 'v' by a single edge.

For example, in Figure 1, the adjacency list of the node 'F' is {B, D, E, F}.

The graphical representation of a social network is not suitable for putting in a computer for obvious reasons. Even any general graph is represented differently inside a computer. The other two representation methods; the adjacency matrix representation or the adjacency list representation are used for this purpose. The vertex set-edge set representation that we used for the standard mathematical definition is too cumbersome and slow to work with in actual algorithms. For example, in order to find the neighbours of a given vertex, the time complexities of adjacency list representation, the adjacency matrix representation runs and the vertex set-edge set representation run in $O(1)$, $O(n)$ and $O(n^2)$ time respectively. Adjacency matrices are suitable for small graphs, and have some advantages over adjacency lists. For example, in a directed graph G on V if we want to find all the vertices with an edge to a fixed vertex j in the adjacency matrix approach, one just looks at the jth column of an adjacency matrix, whereas things are a bit more complicated with the adjacency list. Also, the rich theory of matrices and their well-established properties can be used when representing a network through adjacency matrix.

But, for large graphs, the adjacency list representation is typically far superior in practice, particularly for sparse graphs, i.e., graphs with relatively few edges (closer to n than $n^2$). Social networks tend to be rather sparse. So, while dealing with small size networks the adjacency matrix representation is followed, whereas for large graphs the adjacency list approach is followed by practitioners.

## TYPES OF SOCIAL NETWORKS

There are mainly three types of networks. These are centralized, decentralized and distributed.

- **Centralised Network:** A network in which all other nodes are connected to a single node in the network is called a centralized network. Figure 6 represents a centralised network.
- **Decentralized Network:** A network has small centralized components whose central nodes are connected to each other.
- **Distribute Network:** It is a network in which all the nodes have similar degrees.

*Figure 6. A centralised network*

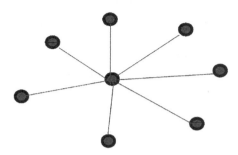

*Figure 7. A decentralised network*

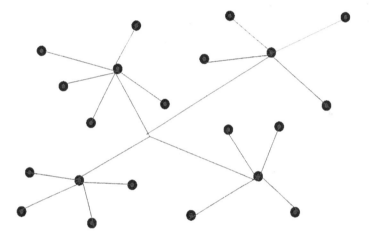

*Figure 8. A distributed network*

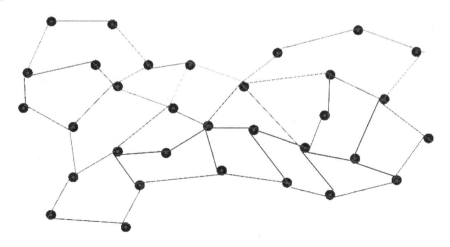

## SECURITY IN SOCIAL NETWORKS

Most social network users share a large amount of their private information in their social network space. This information ranges from demographic information, contact information, comments, images, videos etc. Many users publish their information publicly without careful consideration. Hence social networks have become large pools of sensitive data. Because of their size, huge storage of information and simple accessibility social networks has become new targets that attract cyber criminals. Social networks now a day are based on providing facilities to users like; personal space management, social connection management, connectivity to other applications, social search and social traversal.

Social network security is closely connected with the privacy of the respondents. So, any attack on a social network directly threatens its security and indirectly leads to the violation of privacy of the actors.

## PRIVACY IN SOCIAL NETWORKS

Privacy is the security service provided against the illegal disclosure of information of a person, a product or a company and against exploiting their private information. The more sensitive the information revealed by a user, the higher his privacy risk. If we are able to measure the sensitivity and visibility of a data item exposed in social network site, the control measure to an adequate level can be applied.

The concepts which are necessary to explain the security and privacy of a social network are standard services of security like; confidentiality, integrity and availability. Illegal disclosure and improper use of users' private information may cause undesirable or damaging consequences in the lives of the actors.

Cyber criminals exploit sensitive data and chain of connection mostly through social engineering and reverse social engineering (RSE). The goal of these two methods is to obtain users' context information. Both the methods are being used prior to other attacks such as phishing, spamming and malware attack. In social engineering, attackers approach users' accounts and extract context information to increase successfulness of their attacks. On the other hand, in RSE, they use user's initiative to start a contact and through them influence other actors for performing some actions. The three types of reverse engineering approaches are:

- Recommendation based RSE
- Demographic based RSE
- Visitor-tracking based RSE

In recommendation based RSE, the attackers use the friend recommendation feature to introduce themselves to the victims

In demographic based RSE, the demographic information like, their location and interests are collected through the users.

In visitor-tracking based RSE, depends upon the visitor-tracking feature of some social websites. In this approach the attackers find the users who have viewed the profiles of a corresponding user and track them before visiting their profiles.

## Types of Attacks

There are several types of attacks in prevalence in social networks. These are detailed below.

- **Security Threats:** Due to misuse of social networking services, fake profiles can be generated or actors can be harassed. This may lead to life risks or defamation of the users.
- **Risk for Child Safety:** The social network services can be misused by child and teenagers, particularly with respect to online social harassments.
- **Trolling:** It is an action of abusing individuals emotionally. It can occur in many different forms, like; defacement of tribute pages of deceased person, playing online pranks on volatile individuals and controversial comments. This may cause anger or emotional pain in individuals.
- **Digital Profile Aggregation:** The profiles of various actors can be downloaded and stored and can be used under different contexts. Modulations of these data, which can be stored safely lead to incorrect and irrelevant.
- **Network-Based Risks:** Since free trafficking is allowed in social networks, unsolicited messages (spam), cross site posting (CSS0, viruses and worms can take advantage of this. This may lead to injection of phishing links. CSS attacks and threats are due to widgets (standalone application that can be embedded into a third party sites by any user on a page where they have rights of authorships).

- **Cyber-Stalking:** It is a threatening behaviour, in which attackers repeatedly contact victims by electronic means such as e-mail, Instant messenger and messaging on social networks,
- **Sybil Attacks:** This is an attack in which an user takes on multiple identities and pretends to be multiple and creates distinct nodes called Sybil nodes or Sybil identities in the system. This can be controlled by establishing a trusted central authority that issues and verifies credentials unique to an actual actor. However, this is tedious and many times impractical.

## Privacy Information of Individuals

The pieces of information which are considered an private to individuals in a social network are categorized as follows.

- **Vertex Existence:** Existence of an individual in a social network is considered as privacy of that individual. Useful information can be derived by knowing whether an individual is in the network or not.
- **Vertex Properties:** Some properties of vertices in a social network is considered as its privacy; like the degree of the vertex or its position in the network.
- **Sensitive Vertex Labels:** In a vertex labelled social network, the labels of the nodes can be sensitive or non-sensitive. The sensitive vertex labels are considered as the privacy of the nodes.
- **Link Relationship:** A link between two nodes reflects that they are related to each other with respect to some relation. It is considered as privacy of the two nodes involved.
- **Link Weight:** In many of the social networks the links are having weights, which define the strengths of the relationships. It shows the frequency of association of the concerned nodes.
- **Sensitive Edge Labels:** In some social networks the edges also carry some weights. These are similar to vertex labels. So, these labels can be characterised into sensitive or non-sensitive labels. The sensitive labels are privacy of the concerned nodes.
- **Graph Metrics:** There are several metrics proposed for the social network graphs; like closeness, centrality, reachability and Betweenness. All these metrics are considered as privacy for some individuals. We have already defined these concepts at length in this chapter.

## SOME SOCIAL NETWORKS IN REAL LIFE

There are several social networks which are used in day to day life by most of us. Some of these are; Friendster, Facebook, Myspace and LinkedIn. We shall discuss here on these application social networks briefly.

### Friendster

It is the first popular social networking site based in Kuala Lumpur, Malaysia that allows people to explicitly articulate their social network, present themselves through profile such as interests and demographics, post public testimonials about one another and browse a network of people. It allows people to negotiate context when presenting them. Friendster has more than 80 million of registered user of which the majority of the users are in Asia. Friendster aims to provide a user friendly, highly interactive site so as to enable its users to form and maintain their worldwide connections. It was first launched on 2002 by Johnathan Abrams in Mountain View, California, and was privately owned.

### Facebook

It is a social networking site that began with a focus on colleges and universities, has been studied and evaluated by several workers. Some studies have revealed that Facebook members reveal a lot of information about them, and they are not aware of privacy options or controls who can actually view their profile. It is an American for-profit corporation and an online social media and social networking service based in Menlo Park, California. It was founded in 2004, Cambridge, Massachusetts, United States. The founders had initially limited the website's membership to Harvard students, but since 2006, anyone age 13 and older has been allowed to become a registered user of Facebook. Facebook may be accessed by a large range of desktops, laptops, tablet computers, and smartphones over the Internet and mobile networks.

### Myspace

It is the largest social networking site in the world and mainly focuses on music and popular culture. The use of this site has been prohibited by several schools for their students with a claim that it is a space for cyber criminals. It is a social networking website offering an interactive, user-submitted network of friends, personal profiles, blogs, groups, photos, music, and videos. It is headquartered in Beverly Hills, California. It was founded in 2003.

## LinkedIn

LinkedIn is a business and employment oriented social networking service that operates via websites and mobile apps. It was founded in 2002, and launched in May 2003. It is mainly used for professional networking, including employers posting jobs and job seekers posting their CVs. As of April 2017, LinkedIn had 500 million members in 200 countries. LinkedIn allows members (both workers and employers) to create profiles and "connections" to each other in an online social network which may represent real-world professional relationships. Members can invite anyone (whether an existing member or not) to become a connection. The "gated-access approach" (where contact with any professional requires either an existing relationship or an introduction through a contact of theirs) is intended to build trust among the service's members.

## YouTube

YouTube was founded by Chad Hurley, Steve Chen and Jawed Karim, who were all early employees of PayPal in the early months of 2005. YouTube offers users the ability to view its videos on web pages outside their website. Each YouTube video is accompanied by a piece of HTML that can be used to embed it on any page on the Web. This functionality is often used to embed YouTube videos in social networking pages and blogs. Users wishing to post a video discussing, inspired by or related to another user's video are able to make a "video response". From 2013 onwards, Embedding, rating, commenting and response posting can be disabled by the video owner in YouTube.

YouTube does not usually offer a download link for its videos, and intends for them to be viewed through its website interface. A small number of videos can be downloaded as MP4 files. Numerous third-party web sites, applications and browser plug-ins allow users to download YouTube videos.

## Twitter

It is an online news and social networking service where users post and interact with messages, "tweets", restricted to 140 characters. Registered users can post tweets, but those who are unregistered can only read them. Users access Twitter through its website interface, SMS or a mobile device app. Twitter, Inc. is based in San Francisco, California, United States, and has more than 25 offices around the world.

Twitter was created in March 2006 by Jack Dorsey, Noah Glass, Biz Stone, and Evan Williams and launched in July of that year. The service rapidly gained worldwide popularity. In 2012, more than 100 million users posted 340 million tweets a day, and the service handled an average of 1.6 billion search queries per day. In 2013, it was one of the ten most-visited websites and has been described as "the SMS of the Internet". As of 2016, Twitter had more than 319 million monthly active users. As a social network, Twitter revolves around the principle of followers. When one chooses to follow another Twitter user that user's tweets appear in reverse chronological order on your main Twitter page.

## CONCLUSION

Social networks are used by almost all of us in various forms in different situations. After the advent of online social networks it has become a household name. In this chapter we have introduced the fundamentals of social networks in the form of their representations, types, security aspects and privacy. The danger on publishing the social networks is the danger of the leakage of sensitive information of individuals. These are termed as attacks. We described various types of social network attacks. Social networks contain information about Individuals, out of these some are private and others are not. The respondents do not want that their private information be disclosed. We discussed about privacy information of individuals. Finally, some of the popular social networks which are used in real world scenario are presented.

# REFERENCES

Deo, N. (1974). *Graph Theory, Graph Theory with Applications to Engineering and Computer Science*. Upper Saddle River, NJ: Prentice Hall International, Prentice-Hall, Inc.

Hanneman, R. A. (1998). *Introduction to Social Network Methods*. Riverside, CA: University of California.

Harary, F. (1960). *Graph Theory*. Reading, MA: Addison-Wesley Publishing Company.

Wassermann, S., & Faust, K. (1994). *Social Network Analysis*. Cambridge, UK: Cambridge University Press. doi:10.1017/CBO9780511815478

# Chapter 2
# Social Network Anonymization

## ABSTRACT

*Due to technological advances, it has become easy to collect electronic records from a social network for an adversary. However, the organisations which collect data from social networks have two options before them: either they can publish the data and bear the undesirable consequence of privacy threats or not make it public by avoiding further analysis of these data by social scientists to uncover useful facts, which can be of high importance for the society. Since both these options are undesirable, one can try to find an intermediate way between the two, that is, the data before publishing can be anonymised such that even if an adversary gets some information from the published network, he/she cannot decipher and obtain sensitive information about any individual. By anonymization, the authors mean the perturbation of the real data in order to make it undecipherable. This chapter explores social network anonymization.*

## INTRODUCTION

Due to technological advances, it has become easy to collect electronic records from a social network for an adversary. However, the organisations which collect data from social networks have two options before them; either they can publish the data and bear the undesirable consequence of privacy threats or do not make it public by avoiding further analysis of these data by social scientists to uncover useful facts, which can be of high importance for the society. Since both these options are undesirable, one can try to find out an

DOI: 10.4018/978-1-5225-5158-4.ch002

intermediate way between the two. That is, the data before publishing can be anonymised such that even if an adversary gets some information from the published network, he/she cannot decipher and obtain sensitive information about any individual. By anonymization, we mean the perturbation of the real data in order to make it undecipherable.

An adversary may intrude privacy of some victims using the published social network and some background knowledge. Since most of the social network data come from popular sources like the e-mails, telephone conversations and messages, users expect the privacy of such data. By publishing social network data, it is not enough to protect the privacy if the identifying attributes are replaced with random identifiers.

## SOCIAL NETWORK DATA ANONYMIZATION FACTORS

Privacy preservation of data in social networks is far more challenging than that in relational data. Most of the research done for privacy preservation in data is applicable to relational data only. Since structural relationships of actors are prevalent in social networks, the relational data algorithms cannot be applied to social networks without substantial modifications. Of course, if we collect the information at the nodes of a social network we get a relational database, the tuples being the information about the nodes. Even if we apply anonymisation algorithms to this database, although the characteristic values of the nodes will not be identified, an intruder always has a chance of identifying a node from its structural properties; like their different centralities and degrees. The anonymisation procedures for the relational databases, if used for social networks, would lead to partial anonymisation only. Link anonymisation techniques are thus to be developed. The combination of these two may lead to some anonymisation procedures for social networks. Thus anonymizing social network data is much more challenging than anonymizing relational data.

One of the most important factors which need to be handled is the background knowledge (information that is essential to understanding a situation or problem) of the adversaries. Many pieces of information can be used to identify individuals, such as labels of vertices and edges, neighbourhood graphs, induced subgraphs and their combinations.

The other important factor is the measuring of information loss in anonymizing social network. It is hard to compare two social networks by comparing the vertices and edges individually. The connections come into play. A set of vertices and a set of edges can be connected to form a network in different manners. The connectivity, the Betweenness and diameter can be different. So, measuring the information loss due to anonymisation is not an easy job. Addition or deletion of edges and vertices leads to information loss or addition of redundant and unnecessary information.

Three aspects are very much essential to be remembered while developing protection techniques against privacy attacks. These are; identification of privacy information which are to be protected, modelling of background knowledge of an adversary which can be utilized while attacking the privacy of an individual actor and the published network after anonymization should retain most of its utility.

## Two Useful Properties in Social Network Anonymisation

The following two properties of social networks are useful in devising the anonymisation algorithms.

### Vertex Degree in Power Law Distribution

The degrees of vertices in a large social network follow power law (PL) distribution, that is, only a small number of vertices have a high degree. Processing the higher degree vertices first can keep the information loss about these vertices low. Often, there are many vertices of lower degrees. It is relatively easier to anonymise those lower degree vertices and retain high quality. Some authors state that PLs are simply statistical phenomenon. Some others say these are very interesting tool to analyze data. But, these are to be supported with analytical validation. These are also called as Pareto-like laws; because Pareto in 1896 introduced a distribution to describe income. It showed that the relative number of individuals with an annual income larger than a certain value x was proportional to a power of x. PLs basically tell us that the size of an event is inversely proportional to its frequency. Other applications of PLs in real world contexts include word frequencies, scientific production by chemists and physicists, in studies of number of in and out degrees in models of dynamically growing web graphs, the number of hits in web pages, distribution of biological species, earthquake, rainfall etc. It has been observed that proving the existence of a PL behaviour in natural or human made systems can be very difficult (Wassermann & Faust, 1994).

## Small-World Phenomenon

This phenomenon states that large practical social networks often have surprisingly small average diameters. Anonymisation can be done in the following two ways, both of which involve some information loss. To briefly recapitulate what we discussed in that earlier chapter, the first significant empirical study of the small-world phenomenon was undertaken by the social psychologist Stanley Milgram, who asked randomly chosen "starter" individuals to each try forwarding a letter to a designated "target" person living in the town of Sharon, MA, a suburb of Boston. He provided the target's name, address, occupation, and some personal information, but stipulated that the participants could not mail the letter directly to the target; rather, each participant could only advance the letter by forwarding it to a single acquaintance that he or she knew on a first-name basis, with the goal of reaching the target as rapidly as possible. Roughly a third of the letters eventually arrived at the target, in a median of six steps, and this has since served as basic experimental evidence for the existence of short paths in the global friendship network, linking all (or almost all) of us together in society. This style of experiment, constructing paths through social networks to distant target people, has been repeated by a number of other groups in subsequent decades. Milgram's experiment really demonstrated two striking facts about large social networks: first, that short paths are there in abundance; and second, that people, acting without any sort of global "map" of the network, are effective at collectively finding these short paths. It is easy to imagine a social network where the first of these is true but the second isn't — a world where the short paths are there, but where a letter forwarded from thousands of miles away might simply wander from one acquaintance to another, lost in a maze of social connections (Wassermann & Faust, 1994).

## Modelling of Background Knowledge of Adversaries

Due to the complex structure of the social networks graph, several models have been suggested to capture the background knowledge of adversaries.

- **Identifying Attributes of Vertices:** This is similar to the case for relational data. Like the case of relational data, where a set of attributes act as quasi-identifiers, in this case also a set of attributes, which are modelled as labels can be used to identify a node.

- **Vertex Degrees:** The degree of a vertex states about the number of nodes in the network directly related to the specific node. It is not difficult for an adversary to find out this information and hence re-identify the victim.
- **Link Relationship:** Knowledge regarding any specific mode of communication between groups of individuals can help an adversary to re-identify the victim and its linked nodes.
- **Neighbourhoods:** If an adversary has the knowledge about the neighbourhood of some targeted nodes then it can re-identify the victim by searching vertices in the social graph whose neighbourhood has a clique of the desired size or more. Even the concept of d-neighbourhood can also be used for this purpose.
- **Embedded Subgraphs:** This can be done before the publication of the network, when an adversary can embed some specific subgraphs into it. If it happens that the subgraph embedded is unique in the released network then it can be re-identified.
- **Graph Metrics:** As discussed in chapter 1, there are several metrics for a graph and background knowledge about these can be utilised by the adversary to identify the targeted individuals.

## Categories of Anonymization Methods

The anonymization methods available for social network data can be broadly categorised into clustering based approaches and graph modification approaches.

- **Clustering Based Approaches:** In this category, the vertices or the edges or the vertex attributes are clustered. These clusters are replaced with a super-vertex, so that the details of individual vertices are hidden.
- **Graph Modification Approaches:** Under this approach existing edges or vertices are deleted or additional edges or noise nodes are added to the graph. There are three different ways in which it can be done; optimization approach (where an optimized configuration is determined and the graph is modified accordingly), randomized graph modification approach (basically depend upon perturbation) and greedy graph modification approach (the modifications are introduced depending upon local requirements).

However, in the process of anonymisation it is kept in mind that the utility of the graph is to be maintained to the best possible.

# CLUSTERING BASED APPROACHES

As mentioned in the above sub section, clustering of data in a social network can be achieved through four approaches; vertex clustering, edge clustering, vertex-edge clustering and vertex-Attribute mapping clustering (Hay, Miklau, Jensen, & Towsley, 2008). All these are followed by replacement of the clusters by super nodes to anonymize the node level information and thus reducing the re-identification.

## Vertex Clustering Methods

This approach is followed in Zheleva and Getoor (2007), where an unlabelled graph model was considered. Their method was to take care of vertex identifier attacks and a vertex clustering approach was introduced. Also, the background knowledge of an attacker is categorised into three models, in the form of queries. These are vertex refinement queries, subgraph queries and hub fingerprint queries. Formalism for structural indistinguishability of a vertex with respect to an adversary with external information about the local neighbourhood of the vertex was introduced. The three types of queries are as follows:

- **Vertex Refinement Queries:** This type of queries form a class where the ith level query of a vertex 'v' depends upon the (i-1)th level queries on all the vertices adjacent to 'v'. As the level of a query increases its power of attack also increases. For example; the $0^{th}$ level query returns the level of 'v', the first level query returns the degree of 'v' and so on.
- **Subgraph Queries:** These types of queries assert the existence of a subgraph around the target vertex. The number of edges in the subgraph provides a measure of its descriptive power. An adversary is able to gather a fixed number of edges in a subgraph around a target vertex. The existence of such a subgraph can be expressed as a query and an answer to such a query models the knowledge of the adversary.
- **Hub Fingerprint Queries:** A hub is defined as a vertex in a network with high degree and high Betweenness centrality. A hub fingerprint

for a target vertex 'v' is defined as the vector of distances between 'v' and a set of hubs. The queries model the connections of a vertex to a set of hubs in the network.

The anonymisation scheme proposed in Hay, Miklau, Jensen, and Towsley, (2008) by collecting structurally similar vertices which are indistinguishable to an adversary to form a cluster. It publishes the generalised network obtained by replacing a cluster of vertices by a higher level vertex such that information like the number of vertices in it, the density of edges within and across clusters are stored along with it. It makes the anonymised generalised graph useful to the data scientists as they can study the macro properties of the original graph by studying the properties of the generalised graph.

## Edge Clustering Methods

Zheleva and Getoor have proposed a different type of social network model, which is more general than the standard social network model. They have assumed that the anonymized data will be useful only if it contains both structural properties and node attributes. They have insisted on the relationship between nodes to be kept private in addition to the privacy of nodes. It is considered that the exposure of these relationships is also a privacy breach. The process of finding sensitive relationship from anonymized graphs is called as link re-identification.

An adversary succeeds when it can correctly figure out whether a sensitive edge exists between two vertices. In order to model data utility, the authors proposed to count the number of observations which have to be deleted during the anonymisation process. The smaller the number of removed observations, the higher is the utility.

Several anonymisation strategies are proposed to protect sensitive relationships. These are

- To remove the sensitive edges and keep all other observed edges intact.
- Remove some observed edges. These observed edges are selected as those, say significantly contributing to overall likelihood of a sensitive relationship or those which meet a specific criterion.

The above two approaches lower the utilisation of the anonymised graphs. The authors have suggested for partitioning the node set into equivalence classes basing upon some existing relationship data clustering method and then replacing each cluster by a single vertex and decide which of the edges connecting nodes in two different clusters are to be kept in the generalised graph. One such approach is to publish for each edge type the number of edges of such type between the two equivalence classes of vertices. This approach is called the cluster-edge anonymization. It has some differences from that proposed in Zheleva and Getoor (2007). In the later approach grouping of edges of specific types is used to hide the sensitive relationships, whereas in the approach in Pearl (1988) the vertex identities are kept hidden.

## Vertex and Edge Clustering Methods

Campan and Truta (2008) also take a network generalization approach to the process of anonymizing a social network. Their greedy algorithm optimizes a utility function using the attribute and structural information simultaneously rather than as a two-step process. They introduce a structural information loss measure, and adopt an existing measure of attribute information loss. The anonymization algorithm can be adjusted to preserve more of the structural information of the network or the nodes' attribute values.

The model of social network considered in Zheleva and Getoor (2007) is a simple undirected graph. Vertices in the network are associated with some attributes. The key attributes are removed before anonymization, which is the strategy prevalent in relational data anonymization. The quasi-identifiers, which can be used for re-identification by adversaries and sensitive attributes, are considered as privacy information. Another assumption in Zheleva and Getoor (2007) is that the edges are not labelled. The information loss occurs when the vertices are generalised and structural properties are changed. The relational k-anonymity model is used for clustering of vertices. Their process of anonymizations tries to maintain the originality of attribute values associated with the nodes and also the structure of the network. The method of generalisation is used to anonymize the node clusters. The measure of information loss takes care of both the information loss at the node level and the modification of the original structure. The vertices are labelled with the number of vertices in the cluster and the number of edges.

## Vertex-Attribute Mapping Clustering Methods

A bipartite graph $G = (V, E)$, is such that V can be divided into two sets $V_1$ and $V_2$ where $V = V_1 \cup V_2$ such that $V_1 \cap V_2 = \phi$ and all the edges are connecting one vertex in $V_1$ to another vertex in $V_2$. Cormode et al. (2008) focused on the problem of anonymizing bipartite graphs. The vertices in the two sets $V_1$ and $V_2$ are clustered into groups. The mapping between the groups in the original graph and the published graph are released. Two types of attacks are considered in Cormode et al. (2008) These are, static attacks and learned link attacks. If a group of vertices X in $V_1$ are connected to a set of vertices Y in $V_2$, a static attack can obtain those vertices, which the vertices in X are connected to. This is termed as static attack. On the other hand if very few vertices in X are connected to some vertices not in Y then a learned link attack can obtain the vertices to which vertices in X are connected to with high confidence. A static attack can immediately obtain the vertices that those in X connect to. On the other hand a learned link attack can obtain the vertices that those in X connect to with a high confidence.

In Cormode et al. (2008), the safe grouping mechanism was used to protect privacy. A partition of the vertices of a bipartite graph is said to be a safe grouping if two vertices in the same group in V have no common neighbours in W and vice versa. A (h, k) - safe grouping ensures that each group in V contains at least h vertices and each group in W contains at least k vertices. The algorithm comes under the greedy category as the vertices are processed one by one and for each vertex the algorithm checks whether it can be put in any existing group or a new group is formed. If at the end of the first round some of the groups have less than k elements then the algorithm is run for larger group size and the process is continued.

## GRAPH MODIFICATION APPROACH

We present some of these methods in the following subsections.·

### Optimization Graph Construction Methods

In Liu and Terzi (2008), k-degree anonymization algorithm was introduced. The assumption in this study is that, an adversary is assumed to know the degree of a target victim. By searching the degrees of vertices in the published network, the adversary may be able to identify the individual, even when the identities of the vertices are removed before the network data is published. Several graph properties like; clustering coefficient, average path length and edge intersection are considered as utility of the networks.

The k-degree anonymity followed in this approach is similar to that used for relational data. So, a graph is said to be k-degree anonymous if for every vertex 'v' there are at least (k-1) other vertices in the graph with degree same as 'v'. The identity of 'v' therefore cannot be identified beyond a probability of 1/k.

The notion of degree sequence of a graph G introduced here states it as a sequence of vertices in the degree descending order. A degree sequence is said to be k-degree-anonymous if for every vertex, there are at least (k-1) other vertices having the same degree.

The procedure of anonymisation is carried out in 2 steps; starting from an original degree sequence d, construct a new degree sequence d' such that d' is k-degree anonymous and minimises the degree anonymisation cost and a graph G' is constructed such that d' is the degree sequence of G' such that the edge set E' of G' contains all the edges in edge set E of G. The construction process follows a randomised scheme.

## Randomised Edge Construction Methods

In this method an anonymised graph G' is constructed from the graph G by first deleting a specific number of edges from G and then adding the same number of edges to it. The deletion and addition of edges are done at random from the existing edges and non-existing edges of G. No change in the vertices occurs during these processes. An adversary may try to re-identify individuals with a set of vertices representing its background knowledge. But foe this it has to try for all perturbed graphs obtained from G' by deleting and adding same number of edges from and into it, where the exact number is not known (Hay, Miklau, Jensen, & Towsley, 2008).

## Randomised Spectrum Preserving Methods

This approach is similar to that mentioned above in *Randomised Edge Construction Methods*. They used the concept of spectrum of a graph, which is defined as the set of eigenvalues of the adjacency matrix of the graph. If the adjacency matrix is represented by A, then the eigenvalues are the solutions of the equation $\det(A - \lambda I) = 0$, where I is the unit matrix of the same size as A (Ying & Wu, 2008).

The eigenvalues of a network are connected to important topological properties such as diameter, presence of cohesive clusters, Long paths, bottlenecks and randomness of the graph. So, the spectrum property has close links to topological properties. The anonymisation process is to construct another graph from the original one such that there are very little changes in one or more of the eigenvalues. This in turn confirms the iota of changes in the original graph is not that significant which maintains its utility value. This approach outperforms the edge perturbation approaches (Ying & Wu, 2008).

## Randomised Weight Perturbation Methods

In a weighted graph, the edge weights may be sensitive, which may reflect sensitive relationship between a pair of nodes. With an aim to keep the length of shortest paths being preserved, a Gaussian matrix with mean 0 and standard deviation $\sigma$ was used to perturb the edge weight such the above property is maintained. In another approach, which a greedy approach cannot keep same shortest paths in some cases and in other cases approximate the shortest path lengths (Liu, Wang, Liu, & Zhang, 2008).

Three categories of edges considered:

- **Non-Betweenness Edges:** Those, which are not in any shortest paths of the graph
- **All-Betweenness Edges:** All shortest paths pass through these edges
- **Partial-Betweenness Edges:** Only some of the shortest paths pass through these edges

Depending upon the category of edges, different weight modifications can be applied. So, the approach applies the modifications greedily until a privacy preservation requirement is achieved.

## CONCLUSION

In this chapter we discussed on different social network data anonymisation factors. Two useful properties in social network anonymisation are stated. The adversaries may have some information about the individuals in the network, which may help them in identify the actors. These are called their background knowledge. We discussed on how these background knowledge can be modelled. Clustering methods are popular in anonymizing databases as well as social networks. We discussed on various clustering based methods in social network anonymisation. The other important technique used in social network anonymisation is the graph modification approach. We have presented different methods coming under this category.

## REFERENCES

Agrawal, R., Srikant, R., & Thomas, D. (2005). Privacy preserving olap. In *Proceedings of the 2005 ACM SIGMOD International Conference on Management of Data (SIG-MOD'05)* (pp. 251-262). New York, NY: ACM. doi:10.1145/1066157.1066187

Campan, A., & Truta, T. M. (2008). A clustering approach for data and structural anonymity in social networks. In *Proceedings of the 2nd ACM SIGKDD International Workshop on Privacy, Security, and Trust in KDD(PinKDD'08), in Conjunction with KDD'08*. Las Vegas, NV: ACM.

Cormode, G., Srivastava, D., Yu, T., & Zhang, Q. (2008). Anonymizing bipartite graph data using safe groupings. In *Proceedings of the 34th International Conference on Very Large Databases (VLDB'08)*, ACM. doi:10.14778/1453856.1453947

Evmievski, A., Gehrke, J., & Srikant, R. (2003). Limiting privacy breaches in privacy preserving data Mining. In *Proceedings of the twenty-second ACM SIGMOD-SIGACT-SIGART symposium on Principles of database systems (PODS'03)* (pp. 211-222). New York: ACM. doi:10.1145/773153.773174

Hay, M., Miklau, G., Jensen, D., & Towsley, D. (2008). Resisting structural identification in anonymized social net-works. In *Proceedings of the 34th International Conference on Very Large Databases (VLDB'08)*. ACM.

Liu, K., & Terzi, E. (2008). Towards identity anonymization on graphs. In *Proceedings of the 2008 ACM SIGMOD International Conference on Management of Data (SIG-MOD'08)* (pp. 93-106). New York: ACM Press. doi:10.1145/1376616.1376629

Liu, L., Wang, J., Liu, J., & Zhang, J. (2008). Privacy preserving in social networks against sensitive edge disclosure (Technical Report Technical Report CMIDAHiPSCCS 006-08). Department of Computer Science, University of Kentucky.

Pearl, J. (1988). *Probabilistic reasoning in intelligent systems: networks of plausible inference*. San Francisco, CA: Morgan Kaufmann Publishers Inc.

Tao, Y., Xiao, X., Li, J., & Zhang, D. (2008). On anti-corruption privacy preserving publication. *Proceedings of the 24th International Conference on Data Engineering (ICDE'08)*, 725-734.

Wassermann, S., & Faust, K. (1994). *Social Network Analysis*. Cambridge, UK: Cambridge University Press. doi:10.1017/CBO9780511815478

Ying, X., & Wu, X. (2008). Randomizing social networks: A spectrum preserving approach. In *Proceedings of the 2008 SIAM International Conference on Data Mining (SDM'08)* (pp. 739-750). SIAM. doi:10.1137/1.9781611972788.67

Zheleva, E., & Getoor, L. (2007). Preserving the privacy of sensitive relationships in graph data. *Proceedings of the 1st ACM SIGKDD Workshop on Privacy, Security, and Trust in KDD (PinKDD'07)*.

# Chapter 3
# Social Network
# Anonymization Techniques

## ABSTRACT

*The neighbourhood attack is one of the most significant attacks for disclosing privacy of nodes in a social network. In this chapter, the authors introduce a three-phase anonymization algorithm to tackle this attack. This three-phase algorithm is based upon a similar algorithm introduced earlier for relational data. It takes care of l-diversity anonymisation of a database. Also, a latest algorithm in this direction, called GASNA, is presented in detail. The concept of partial anonymity is introduced and its importance is explained.*

## INTRODUCTION

In the previous chapter we have talked about anonymization of social networks and some general approaches for that. In this chapter we shall move into some detail of specific anonymization techniques. In fact, we shall be considering an anonymisation procedure to prevent neighbourhood attack and the other one being a greedy algorithm for social network anonymisation. In order to explain the concept of background knowledge and how it can help an adversary in identifying a respondent in a social network let us consider the following situation.

Let us consider the social network of friends given in Figure 1. The anonymised network is given in Figure 2. Suppose, an adversary knows that F has four friends. Even though the network is anonymised, it can be

DOI: 10.4018/978-1-5225-5158-4.ch003

*Figure 1. A friend network*

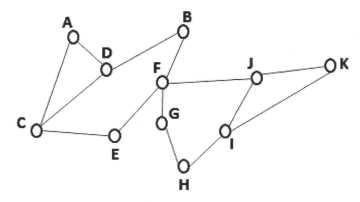

*Figure 2. The network with anonymous nodes*

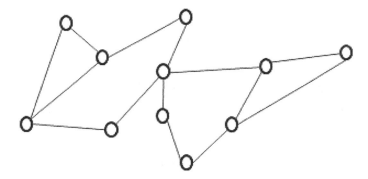

observed that there is only one node in Figure 2 having degree 4, B can be identified by the adversary. So, through the 1-neighbourhood graph helps in this identification. Of course, the background knowledge plays an important role here. In this chapter we shall discuss on the anonymisation algorithms which can provide security against neighbourhood attacks.

## ANONYMISATION AGAINST NEIGHBOURHOOD ATTACK

First we shall present the anonymisation techniques used for privacy preservation against neighbourhood attacks.

The concept of level hierarchy was used by Zhou and Pei (2008) for developing an anonymisation technique to prevent neighbourhood attacks. There is a meta symbol * generalising all levels. Other levels are arranged downward manner from general ones to specific one.

We recall the definition of a neighbourhood, which is as follows:

**Definition 1:** In a social network G, the neighbourhood of a vertex 'u' is the inducedsubgraphoftheneighboursofu,denotedby $Neighbour_G(u) = G(N_u)$, where $N_u = \{v \mid (u,v) \in E\}$.

The components of the neighbourhood graph of a vertex are the neighbourhood components. In a social network G, a subgraph C of G is a neighbourhood component of $u \in V$ if C is a maximal connected subgraph in $Neighbour_G(u)$.

**Definition 2:** The d-neighbourhood graph of a vertex 'u' includes all the vertices that are within the distance d from the vertex u.

The aim of the anonymisation process in Zhou and Pei (2008) is to enable the anonymised graph to be able to provide answers to aggregate network queries.

**Definition 3:** Two graphs G and H are said to be isomorphic, if there exists a bijection 'f' between the vertices V and W of G and H respectively $f : V \to W$ such that any two vertices u and v of G are adjacent in G if and only if $f$(u) and $f$(v) are adjacent in H.

This kind of bijection is commonly described as "edge-preserving bijection", in accordance with the general notion of isomorphism being a structure-preserving bijection.

To check the isomorphism of two graphs a technique called DFS code is used here. Encoding the edges and vertices in a graph is done on the basis of DFS tree. All the vertices in G can be encoded in the preorder of the DFS tree. However, the DFS tree is generally not unique in a graph. So, the notion of minimum DFS code is used, which is defined as follows:

**Definition 4:** For any connected graph G, let T be a DFS tree of G. Then an edge is always listed as $(v_i, v_j)$ such that i < j. We define a linear ordering over the edges in G denoted by $\prec$, which is defined as follows:

Let $e = (v_i, v_j)$ and $e' = (v_i', v_j')$. We say that $e \prec e'$ if any of the following four cases hold true.

1. When both e and e' are forward edges such that j < j' or (i > i' and j = j')
2. When both e and e' are backward edges such that i < i' or (i = i' and j < j')
3. When e is a forward edge and e' is a backward edge, where $j \leq i'$
4. When e is a backward edge and e' is a forward edge, where I < j'

It can be easily verified that $\prec$ is a linear order on E.

**Definition 5:** For a graph G and a DFS tree T, a list of edges in E in the order $\prec$ is called the DFS code of G with respect to T.

For any two DFS trees $T_1$ and $T_2$ on G, their DFS codes can be compared lexically with the vertex pairs as the labels of edges. The lexically minimum DFS code is selected as the representation of G, denoted by DFS(G).

- **Property:** Two graphs G and G' are isomorphic if and only if DFS(G) = DFS(G').

## Algorithm for Anonymisation of Social Network Against Neighbourhood Attack (Zhou & Pei, 2008)

**Input:** A social network G = (V, E) and the cost function parameters
   **Output:** An anonymised graph G'

1. Initialize G' = G
2. Mark $v_i \in V$ as "unanonymised"
3. Sort $v_i \in V$ as Vertex-List in neighbourhood size descending order
4. While ($VertexList \neq \phi$) Do
5. Let Seed-Vertex = Vertex-List. head() and remove Vertex-List

6.  For each $v_i \in VertexList$ Do
7.  Calculate Cost (Seed Vertex, $v_i$) using the anonymisation method for two vertices
8.  End For
9.  If (Vertex-Listsize() ≥ 2k-1) Do
10. Let CandidateSet contain the top k-1 vertices with the smallest cost
11. Else
12. Let CandidateSet contain the remaining unanonymised vertices
13. Suppose CandidateSet $= \{u_1, u_2, ... u_m\}$, anonymise Neighbour (Seed Vertex) and Neighbour ()
14. For j = 2 to m Do
15. Anonymise Neighbour($u_j$) and Neighbour(Seed Vertex), Neighbour($u_1$), ...Neighbour($u_{j-1}$) be marked as "anonymised"
16. Update VertexList
17. End For
18. End While

An improved version of this algorithm is presented in Tripathy, Lakshmi, and Jain (2009). The social network model is presented in the form of an adjacency matrix. It also introduces and uses a new algorithm for testing isomorphism of graphs, called the revised brute force graph-isomorphism algorithm, which is as follows.

## Revised Brute Force Graph-Isomorphism Algorithm

**Input:** Two graphs G and H
  **Output:** Yes or No depending upon whether the graphs re isomorphic or not

1.  Let $V_G$ and $V_H$ denote the set of vertices of the two graphs G and H respectively
2.  If $V_G \neq V_H$ return No
3.  Else, put the vertices in G and H in the descending orders of their degrees
4.  If degree sequences are not equal return No
5.  Generate the adjacency matrices $A_G$ and $A_H$ of G and H respectively with respect to the ordering of the vertices
6.  Let the number of vertices of order I, I = 1, 2...k in the graphs G and H be $G_{n_i}$ and $H_{n_i}$

7.  For j = k...1
8.  If $G_{n_i} \neq H_{n_i}$ for some I, then return No
9.  Else, let $[A_G]_j$ and $[A_H]_j$, denote the submatrices of $A_G$ and $A_H$ corresponding to the vertices of order j, respectively
10. For a particular ordering of $[A_G]_j$ write $[A_H]_j$ in that order
11. If $[A_G]_j \neq [A_H]_j$ then return No
12. Else, return "Yes"

This algorithm has a complexity advantage over the Brute Force algorithm. If there are n vertices in the two graphs G and H, the Brute Force algorithm is of order $O(n!)$, where the complexity of the revised algorithm is

$$O(n_1! + n_2! + ... + n_k!) = O(n_j!),$$

where $n_j = \max\{n_1, n_2 ... n_k\}$.

## The Revised Network Anonymisation Procedure

1.  For all the vertices of the graph G, the vertices that fall in its d-neighbourhood are considered. The neighbourhood components are obtained for each of the vertex neighbourhood.
2.  First, mark all vertices in the network as "unanonymised". Maintain a list Vertex-List of "unanonymised" vertices according to the descending order of the number of vertices in the neighbourhood. The vertices with the same number of vertices in the neighbourhood are arranged arbitrarily.
3.  Iteratively, we pick the first vertex Seed Vertex in the list Vertex-List. The anonymisation cost of Seed Vertex and any other vertices in Vertex-List is calculated using the anonymisation method for two vertices earlier. If the number of unanonymised vertices in Vertex-List is at least (2k-1), we select a Candidate-Set of the top k-1 vertices in the Vertex-List with the smallest anonymisation cost.
4.  It is not possible that every vertex in a graph can find at least one other vertex with isomorphic neighbourhoods. So, a factor known as "Anonymisation Quality Measure" or "Anonymisation Cost" is calculated for every pair of vertices that do not find a match. The vertices with the minimum cost can be grouped for anonymisation.

5.  The Seed-vertex and the vertices in the Candidate-Set are anonymised in turn using the anonymisation method for two vertices discussed earlier. The anonymisation of Seed vertex and $u_1$ is straight forward. After these two vertices are anonymised their neighbourhoods are identical. When we anonymise them with respect to $u_2$, any change to the neighbourhood of Seed vertex will be applied to $u_1$ as well, so that the neighbourhoods of the Seed Vertex, $u_1$ and $u_2$ are the same. The process continues until the neighbourhoods of Seed vertex and $u_1$, $u_2$, ... $u_m$ are anonymised.

6.  During the anonymisation of a group of vertices, some changes may occur to some other vertices 'v' that have been marked as "anonymised" in another group. In order to maintain the k-anonymity for these vertices, we apply the same changes to every other (k-1) vertices having the isomorphic neighbourhoods as 'v'. Once those k vertices are changed, they are marked as "unanonymised" and inserted into the Vertex-List again.

7.  When the number of unanonymised vertices in Vertex-List is less the 2k, to satisfy the k-anonymity, the remaining vertices in Vertex-List have to be considered together for anonymisation. They are added to the Candidate-Set in a batch. The social network anonymisation algorithm continues until all the vertices in the graph are marked as "anonymised".

## GASNA: A GREEDY ALGORITHM FOR SOCIAL NETWORK ANONYMISATION

This algorithm was specifically developed to provide structural anonymity and protection of sensitive attributes by achieving k-anonymity and l-diversity in social network data. In this algorithm edge addition technique is used. But, the algorithm takes care of adding minimum number of edges for anonymisation.

Previously, a three-phase algorithm was proposed by Tripathy et al. (2010), which incorporated both clustering and graph manipulation. The model prevents target individual identity from attack by an adversary. The authors have used a fast isomorphism technique to identify structurally similar nodes in the graph. In the first phase similar nodes which satisfy k-anonymity and l-diversity are clustered together. The second phase takes care of adjustment of cluster elements to achieve the minimum number of elements in a cluster to be k. The third phase takes care of l-diversity property for sensitive attributes. GASNA is developed basing upon this three phase algorithm.

One of the major advantages of the 3-phase algorithm was that it is applicable for $d \geq 2$. The earlier algorithms, as detailed in section 2 are applicable for d = 1 only. However, the algorithm requires high cost to achieve this. Cost to anonymise a network is directly proportional to the number of edges added to make the network anonymous. Also, no concrete method was provided for addition of edges.

In GASNA, efforts have been made to cross over these hurdles. Following the 3-phase algorithm, it also has three phases; the clustering phase, the adjustment phase and the anonymisation phase.

As noted earlier, a common disadvantage of the techniques used for anonymisation is that the original network is changed after manipulation and consequently, the utility of the graph decreases. To handle such situations, Dwork et al (2014) introduced the concept of differential privacy in the context of networks. Differential privacy is a property of an algorithm. Informally, it requires that an algorithm be insensitive to small changes in the input, such as the addition or removal of a single record. The formal definition uses the concept of neighbouring databases. Two databases D and D' are neighbours of each other if they differ by at most one record; that is if $\left|(D - D') \cup (D' - D)\right| = 1$. As a parallel notion, graphs which differ by a single edge are called as neighbouring graphs. Following this approach, a differentially private algorithm essentially protects against edge disclosure. Differential privacy places no limiting assumptions on the input or on adversary knowledge. An adversary with knowledge of all of the edges in the graph except one cannot use the differentially private algorithm to infer the presence or absence of the unknown target edge.

## Clustering Phase

It takes care of grouping similar nodes together to form clusters. The cost function is used to determine the similarity. The nodes having low similarity cost are grouped together. Earlier algorithms proposed to find out whether two nodes have isomorphic neighbourhoods are costly. So, a new approach was proposed in Shisodia, Jain, & Tripathy (2013).

In order to make the structure of a node x similar to that of a node y for neighbourhood d, the cost of adding an edge at a distance 'dis' from x is (d - dis+1). Let us denote the neighbourhoods of nodes 'x' by X and that of 'y' by Y for d = 1. In order to make X and Y similar, one has to use the neighbourhood similarity.

## Algorithm

**Input:** A set T of n-nodes, the value k for k-anonymity, the value 1 for l-diversity and the value d for d-neighbourhood. Let $T_i$ be the ith node in the input graph

**Output:** Clusters $\{C_1, C_2, ... C_m\}$; $m \geq \lfloor n / (k + l - 1) \rfloor$

1.  Order $\{T_i\}$ according to degrees in descending order. Store this in array Q
2.  Let x = 0 and cid = 0
3.  Mark visited $[T_i] = 0$ $\forall i = 0, 1, 2...(n-1)$ ; j = 0
4.  While (j < n) do
5.  if(visited[Q(j)] =0 then
6.  Add Q[x] to $C_{cid}$
7.  let p = 0, y = x =1 and ca[ ] be ascending cost array
8.  While (y < n) do
9.  if (visited[Q(y)] = 0 and distance(Q[y]. each element in $C_{cid}$ })> d-1) then
10. Calculate cost, i.e. $cost_y$
11. Insert the cost into ca[ ]
12. end
13. for each element in ca[ ] as ca[z] do
14. Let flag = 0
15. while(flag == 0) do
16. Let s($C_{cid}$) be the set of distinct sensitive attribute values of the node in $C_{cid}$
17. Let s[z] be the sensitive attribute value of ca[z]
18. if ($C_{cid}$ <k) or (($s_{[z]} \notin s(C_{id})$) and ($| s(C_{id}) |< l$)) then add $ca_{[z]}$ to $C_{cid}$
19. end
20. if (($C_{cid} \geq$ k) and ($| s(C_{id} \geq l$)) then flag = 1
21. end
22. end
23. end
24. $j^{++}$

25. end
26. end
27. end

## Adjustment Phase

The adjustment phase guarantees that every cluster has at least k nodes. The clusters formed in early iterations of the clustering algorithm have lower chances of having less than k nodes compared to the clusters formed towards the end of clustering phase. This is due to the fact that clusters formed in initial stage of clustering algorithm have enough nodes to satisfy k-anonymity and l-diversity, but the clusters formed in the end may not satisfy this due to scarcity of nodes. The adjustment phase algorithm starts from the last cluster formed. The clusters having less than k nodes are merged together so that the resulting cluster has at least k nodes. If there is only one cluster left with less than k nodes, its nodes re moved to the cluster whose nodes have maximum similarity with respect to that node.

### Algorithm Adjustment Phase

**Input:** Clusters $\{C_1, C_2, ... C_m\}; m \geq \lfloor n / (k + l - 1) \rfloor$

    **Output:** Adjusted clusters with each cluster having a minimum size of k

1.    Let I = m-1
2.    While ($i \geq 0$) do
3.    if ($|C_i| < k$) then
4.    j = i -1
5.    While ($j \geq 0$) do
6.    p = 0
7.    While (p < $|C_j|$) do
8.    Calculate the cluster having elements with maximum similarity with respect to element $C_i[p]$ and shift $C_i[p]$ to that cluster
9.    $p^{++}$
10.    end
11.    end
12.    end

13. $i^{--}$
14. end

## Anonymisation Phase

An anonymised graph is generated. This can be done using the following techniques.

### Edge Addition by Introducing Fake Nodes in the Cluster

In this approach fake nodes are added to the clusters to anonymize the nodes in it. The degree of fake nodes in the graph is taken as the maximum of the most probable degree. This is done to ensure that the average degree of graph and the structural properties of the graph are maintained. New edges are added to connect these fake nodes to the needy nodes in the graph till they do not cross the most probable degree. Edges are selected such that they connect the fake nodes to the codes which require highest degree to achieve anonymity. Finally, edges are added among fake nodes to anonymize them even if they have crossed the most probable degree.

### Edge Addition to Existing Nodes

This is an approach to provide additional degree to the existing nodes. By adding an edge, two degrees are provided to the concerned nodes. If the degree requirement of any node is not satisfied and there are no other nodes in the cluster to which it can be connected then join it to another node in a nearby cluster such that it is connected to a node of odd degree if the node requirement is odd else to a node of even degree. On the contrary, if no such nearby clusters are available with nodes satisfying this property then add fake nodes and connect to them.

### Removal of Edges

If in the above two approaches it is observed that some nodes have more degrees than majority of nodes in their clusters then some extra degrees are reduced by removing edges from these nodes. There is of course a problem with this approach as there can be other nodes connected to these high degree nodes, which will lose degrees and if there are nodes of lower degrees then the process leads to imbalance in the node degrees.

## Algorithm Anonymisation Phase

**Input:** Adjusted clusters with each cluster having a minimum size of k
   **Output:** Anonymised graph

1.   P = degree possessed by maximum number of nodes
2.   Let i = j = c = 0
3.   While (i < m) do
4.   D = max_degree($C_i$)
5.   While (j < |$C_i$|) do
6.   Let da[ ] be 'degree to be added' array; da[c] = D − degree($C_i[j]$); nodes[c] = $C_i[j]$
7.   $c^{++}; j^{++}$
8.   end
9.   $i^{++}$
10.   end
11.   Order nodes[] and da[] according to their corresponding da[] values in descending order
12.   Let $s = \sum_{i=0}^{m} da[i]$
13.   Let a= $\lfloor s / P \rfloor$ and b = da[0], c = max{a, b}
14.   Create an array fn[c] with c fake nodes containing ($\lceil s / P \rceil$ -1) nodes of value $P_d$ and 1 node of value $P_d$ + Smod($P_d$)
15.   i = 0; j = 0
16.   While (j < n) do
17.   if (da[j] == 0) then $j^{++}$ else
18.   if (fn[i] == 0) then I = (i+1) mod(c)
19.   else
20.   Connect node[j] with ith fake node; da[j]--; fn[i]--; i = (i+1) mod(c)
21.   end
22.   end
23.   end

24. least_anonymized_degree = degree (C[m-1][0]); I = c − 1
25. While (i > 0) do
26. j = i − 1
27. While ((P − fn[i]) < lad) do
28. fn[i]—
29. connect fake_node[i] and fake_node[j]; j = (j − 1) modc
30. if (j == i) then break
31. end
32. end
33. i—
34. end

## Empirical Evaluation of GASNA

For empirical evaluation of the performance of this algorithm, it was applied to the social network data generated by recursive matrix (RMAT) (Chakrabarty, Zhan, & Faloutsos, 2004). RMAT generates graphs with power law vertex degree distribution and small world characteristic. R-MAT takes 4 probability parameters, namely a, b, c and d. The default values taken for these parameters in Shisodia, Jain, and Tripathy (2013) were 0.45, 0.15, 0.15 and 0.25 respectively. A series of synthetic datasets were generated by varying the number of vertices between 128 and 4096. The average degree varies from 3 to 7. A list of 32 city names was generated and the names were equally distributed among the nodes. The algorithm was evaluated for 1-neighbourhood. It was observed that there is an increase in the number of edges when the value of l for l-diversity is higher than the value of k for k-anonymity. This happens because when the number of vertices in the cluster reaches k, only those vertices can further be added which have a sensitive attribute value not already present in the cluster. Nodes which are not that similar structurally are added to the cluster to make it l-diverse. The cost increases because of this.

Also, GASNA was applied to real world data by taking the co-authorship network of scientists working on network theory and experiment (Shisodia, Jain, & Tripathy, 2013). The version used contained all components of the network, for a total of 1589 scientists. The sensitive attribute was taken to be the first letter of the first name of a scientist.

A comparative study of GASNA with the algorithms in Wei and Lu (2008), and Zhou and Pei (2008) show that the number edges to be added following GASNA is significantly lower for 5000 nodes. In this comparison GASNA has been applied only for degree-based attacks. As a result the utility of the anonymised graph obtained by using GASNA is better than those in in Wei and Lu (2008), and Zhou and Pei (2008).

## THE NOTION OF PARTIAL ANONYMITY

The nodes of a cluster are said to be partially anonymised if each ith node in the cluster has a neighbourhood structure which is a subset of (i+1) th node neighbourhood structure for a given d-neighbourhood value. The idea of partial anonymity is to make the structure of the ith node in the cluster similar to structure of (i+1)th node in it. If there is a change in the structure of the ith node in order to make it structurally similar to the (i+1)th node then it is not reflected in the (i-1)th node. This reduces the number of edges to be added. However, if there is an addition in the degree of the ith node then it is reflected on all previous nodes.

This concept is yet to utilised in anonymisation algorithms. However, it can be used to a few targeted nodes in a large social network, which are supposed to be more vulnerable than other nodes. In such cases, the complexity of large social network anonymisation will not occur.

## CONCLUSION

In this chapter, we discussed the problem of anonymisation against neighbourhood attack and presented a recently developed efficient algorithm named GASNA. This algorithm enhances an earlier anonymisation algorithm, called the three phase algorithm developed in Tripathy, and Panda (2010). The major improvement in GASNA occurs in the anonymisation phase, where the concepts called edge addition to existing nodes, edge addition for the fake nodes added and removal of edges are used. Finally a passing introduction on partial anonymisation of social networks is introduced, which is subject to further studies.

# REFERENCES

Chakrabarty, D., Zhan, Y., & Faloutsos, C. (2004). *R_MAT: A recursive model for graph mining*. Computer Science Department, Carnegie Mellon University, N0.541.

Dwork, C., & Roth, A. (2014). The algorithmic Foundations of Differential Privacy. *Foundations and Trends in Theoretical Computer Science, 9*(3-4), 211–407. doi:10.1561/0400000042

Horwitz, E., Sahani, S., & Rajasekharan, S. (2004). *Fundamentals of Computer Algorithms. Darya Ganj*. New Delhi, India: Galgotia Publications.

Newman, M. E. (2006). Finding community structure in networks using the eigen vectors of matrices. *Physical Review E, 74*(3).

Shisodia, M., Jain, S., & Tripathy, B. K. (2013). GASNA: A greedy algorithm for social network anonymization. *Proceeding of the 2013 International Conference on Advances in Social Networks Analysis and Mining*.

Tripathy, B. K., Lakshmi, J., & Jain, N. (2009). Security against neighbourhood attacks in social networks. In *Proceedings of the National Conference on Recent Trends in Soft computing* (pp. 216-223). Bangalore, India: Academic Press.

Tripathy, B. K., & Mitra, A. (2012). An algorithm to achieve k-anonymity and l-diversity anonymisation in social networks. *Proceedings on the 2012 Fourth International Conference on Computational Aspects of Social Networks (CASoN)*, 126-131. doi:10.1109/CASoN.2012.6412390

Tripathy, B. K., & Panda, G. K. (2010). A new approach to manage security against neighbourhood attacks in social networks. *Proceedings of the 2010 international conference on Advances in Social Network analysis and Mining*, 264-269. doi:10.1109/ASONAM.2010.69

Wei, Q., & Lu, Y. (2008). Preservation of privacy in publishing social network data. In *Proceedings on the 2008 International Symposium on Electronic Commerce and Security* (pp. 421-425). IEEE. doi:10.1109/ISECS.2008.112

Zhou, B., & Pei, J. (2008). Preserving privacy in social networks against neighbourhood attacks. In *Proceedings on IEEE 24th International Conference on Data Engineering* (pp. 506-515). IEEE.

Chapter 4
# Clustering Approaches

## ABSTRACT

*Clustering-based approaches, also known as generalization approaches, are popular in anonymizing relational data. In social networks, these generalization approaches are applied to vertices and edges of the graph. The vertices and edges are grouped into partitions called super-vertices and super-edges, respectively. In most cases, these vertices and edges are divided according to some predefined loss function. One major drawback of this approach is that the graph shrinks considerably after anonymization, which makes it undesirable for analyzing local structures. However, the details about individuals are properly hidden and the generalized graph can still be used to study macro-properties of the original graph.*

## INTRODUCTION

For better understanding of Clustering approaches, let's look at a small network shown in Figure 1. Its generalized version is given in Figure 2. We have considered 4 super-vertices and the vertices included in each super-vertex is clustered in the original graph.

Arrangement of vertices in clusters is done using a predefined loss function. The clusters are usually labelled by their size and the number of intra-cluster edges present in them. The edges between clusters are labelled by the corresponding number of inter-cluster edges present in the network. Note that the intersection of any two clusters is usually null. A traditional definition of good clustering is that nodes assigned to the same cluster should

DOI: 10.4018/978-1-5225-5158-4.ch004

*Figure 1. A small network*

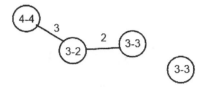

*Figure 2. Generalized version of figure*

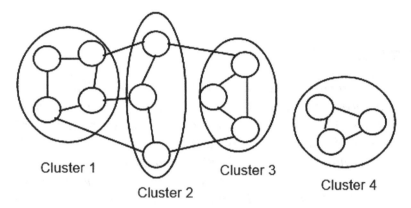

Cluster 1                   Cluster 3                   Cluster 4

Cluster 2

be highly similar and nodes assigned to a different cluster should be highly dissimilar. Number of clusters, minimum size, maximum size, average size all are crucial factors of any clustering algorithm. Various algorithms have been proposed for achieving anonymization through clustering and saNGreeA is the leading algorithm in this field. We shall discuss this algorithm in the section titled *saNGreeA Algorithm*. Clustering-based approaches are divided into four sub-categories: vertex clustering methods, edge clustering methods, vertex and edge clustering methods, and vertex-attribute mapping clustering methods.

# VERTEX CLUSTERING METHODS

Vertex clustering method generalizes an input network by grouping all the vertices into partitions and publishing the number of vertices in each partition along with the number of edges within and across every partition.

# GraphGen Algorithm

Hay et al. (2010) developed an anonymization technique using this approach. Their generalization algorithm called GraphGen takes the original graph and 'k' (the minimum super-vertices size). It outputs a generalized graph whose super-vertices have at least 'k' vertices. Let G = (V, E) be the original graph and Ĝ = (Ṽ, Ɛ) be a generalization of G, then W(Ĝ) is the set of possible worlds (graphs over V) that are consistent with Ĝ. Note that Ṽ are subsets of V and are the nodes of the generalized graph Ĝ. The size of W(Ĝ) is a measure of the accuracy of Ĝ as a summary of G. To find the best fitting generalized graph, the algorithm uses Maximum Likelihood as the fitness function. The probability function is assumed to be uniform over the possible worlds. For a graph g ∈ W(Ĝ), $\Pr_{\hat{G}}[g] = 1/|W(\hat{G})|$ where |W(Ĝ)| is the number of possible worlds.

$$\left|W(\hat{G})\right| = \prod_{X \in \tilde{V}} \binom{\frac{1}{2}|X|(|X|-1)}{d(X,X)} \prod_{X,Y \in \tilde{V}} \binom{|X||Y|}{d(X,Y)}$$

Design of the search algorithm is based on stochastic block-modelling whose main objective is to ensure that nodes in the same group have similar social importance. GraphGen searches for the best generalized graph by using simulated annealing (Russel & Norvig, 2003) Simulated annealing is a method for approximating the global optimum of a given function using probabilistic techniques. It uses a temperature parameter for determining the probability of accepting locally bad decisions. Initially we set the temperature to a high value and it is cooled down gradually. A valid generalized graph is one where every supernode has at least 'k' nodes and each valid generalized graph is a state in the search space. The algorithm starts with a generalized graph that has a single super-vertex containing all the vertices of the graph and proposes a state change by splitting a partition, moving a node to a different partition, or by merging two partitions. The proposal to change the state to create a new generalized graph from the previous one is evaluated based on the change in likelihood that results. The proposal is always accepted if the likelihood is improved and accepted with some probability of likelihood is decreased by the new state. The search is terminated when fewer than 0.02% of the proposals are accepted. Initially, the acceptance probability starts high and is cooled slowly until it approaches zero.

Sometimes, GraphGen returns a partitioning that is only locally maximal. This is partly due to simulated annealing's cooling schedule. Only if the cooling takes place slowly enough, the global maximum will be returned with high probability. However, finding the global optimum is an intractable problem and one cannot quantify how close the output is to the optimum. From the experimental results done in Hay et al. (2010) on the Enron graph with 'k' as 3, the log-likelihood of the output partition ranged from -362.6 to -353.3 compared to a greedy algorithm which returned a partition of only -511.5. More details and design considerations of the GraphGen algorithm can be found in Hay et al. (2010). The GraphGen Algorithm pseudocode is given below:

**Input:** Original Graph G = (V, E), minimum super-vertex size 'k'

**Output:** Generalized graph $\hat{G} = (\tilde{V}, \mathcal{E})$ where every super-vertex has at least 'k' vertices.

1.    $\hat{G} \leftarrow$ Initialize (G) {All nodes in a single partition}
2.    $t_{cycle} \leftarrow 5|V|$
3.    **for** $t \leftarrow 1$ to $\infty$ **do**
4.    $T \leftarrow$ Schedule(t) {Cooling Schedule for Simulated Annealing (T cools as t increases}
5.    $S \leftarrow$ Successors($\hat{G}$, k)
6.    $\hat{G}' \leftarrow$ arg max $_{\hat{G}' \varepsilon S} \dfrac{1}{\left|W\left(\hat{G}'\right)\right|}$ { Find Max Likelihood Successor}
7.    $\Delta L \leftarrow \dfrac{1}{\left|W\left(\hat{G}'\right)\right|} - \dfrac{1}{\left|W\left(\hat{G}'\right)\right|}$ { Change in Likelihood}
8.    **if** $\Delta L > 0$ **then**
9.    $\hat{G} \leftarrow \hat{G}'$
10.   **else**
11.   $\hat{G} \leftarrow \hat{G}'$ with probability $e^{\frac{\Delta L}{T}}$
12.   **if** $\hat{G}$ updated less than 0.02% of last $t_{cycle}$ steps **then**
13.   return $\hat{G}$
14.   **end if**
15.   end for

**Successors:** A subroutine that returns a set of generalized graphs derived from $\hat{G}$ by making a small change such as splitting, merging or moving super-vertices. 'X' and 'Y' are vertices of the generalized graph (super-vertices of the original graph). It takes input as the generalized graph $\hat{G}$ and minimum super-vertex size 'k'. It outputs a set of graphs which are the successors to $\hat{G}$.

1.  $S \leftarrow \emptyset$ {Initialize the set of successors}
2.  $u \leftarrow$ Choose random node
3.  $X \leftarrow$ Find super-vertex that contains u
4.  **if** $|X| > 2k$ **then**
5.  $\hat{G}' \leftarrow$ Split $(X, \hat{G})$ {Choose greedy split of X}
6.  $S \leftarrow \{\hat{G}\}$
7.  end if
8.  **for** Y such that X, Y are neighbors or share a neighbors **do**
9.  **if** $|X| > k$ **then**
10. $\hat{G} \leftarrow$ MoveNode $(u, X, Y, \hat{G})$
11. $S \leftarrow S \cup \{\hat{G}\}$
12. **end if**
13. $\hat{G} \leftarrow$ MergeAndSplit $(X, Y, \hat{G})$
14. $S \leftarrow S \cup \{\hat{G}\}$
15. end for
16. **return** S

An extension to the GraphGen had been proposed by Hay et al. in the same paper, one which considers only the vulnerable vertices so that the structural properties of the graph may be better preserved. To incorporate this extension, we need to identify the vulnerable vertices first. Given an adversary model Q and group size 'k', a vertex x is vulnerable if $|cand_Q (x)| < k$ where $cand_Q$ stands for candidate set under Q. For a given knowledge query Q over a graph, the candidate set of a target node x w.r.t to Q is $cand_Q (x) = \{y \in V \mid Q(x) = Q(y)\}$. In the sample network shown in Figure 3, if

*Figure 3. Sample network for candidate set*

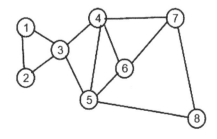

Q is the knowledge query returning the degree of a node and node 3 is our target node then Q (3) = 4 and $cand_Q$ (3) = {3,4,5} which is the set of all vertices whose degree is 4.

The privacy condition of the generalized graph is altered so that only if a super-vertex contains a vulnerable vertex, then its size must be at least 'k'. Therefore, an invulnerable vertex can be placed in a super-vertex of size 1. This relaxed privacy is incorporated in the search procedure by allowing state changes that place invulnerable vertices into super-vertices of size less than 'k'. As an alternate approach, the search can be executed as described above, and then the super-vertices that contain only invulnerable vertices can be replaced with individual super-vertices for each invulnerable vertex. The pseudocode for the modified GraphGen algorithm is given below:

**Input:** G = (V, E) {original graph to generalize}, 'k' {Minimum super-vertex size}, Q {knowledge query representing adversary capability}.

**Output:** Ĝ {A generalized graph that satisfies graph k-anonymity w.r.t Q adversaries.

1.   $S \leftarrow \{u \in V| |cand_Q (x)| < k\}$ {Vulnerable nodes}
2.   $\hat{G} \leftarrow$ GraphGen (G, k)

{Replace super-vertices that contain only invulnerable vertices}

3.   **for** super-vertex X in Ĝ **do**
4.   **if** X ∩ S = Ø **then**
5.   replace X with a super-vertex for each u ∈X
6.   **end if**
7.   **end for**
8.   **return** Ĝ

The GraphGen algorithm had been compared against BKCS algorithm (Cormode, Srivastava, Bhagat, & Krishnamurthy, 2009) and the LT algorithm (Liu & Terzi, 2008). GraphGen and LT perform consistently better than BCKS. LT and GraphGen algorithms are comparable and LT outperforms GraphGen in some metrics.

## Sequential Clustering Algorithm

Sequential clustering Algorithm was first proposed in Goldberger and Tassa (2010) and was adapted for social network anonymization in Tassa and Cohen

(2013). Sequential Clustering is a local search algorithm just like simulated annealing. Simulated annealing is sensitive to the cooling schedule and sequential clustering can be repeated several times with different random partitions as the starting point, to find the best local minimum in those repeated searches. The algorithm is described below:

**Input:** A social network graph $G = (V, E)$ and an integer 'k' (minimum cluster size)

**Output:** A clustering of G into clusters where each cluster size $\geq k$

1. Choose a random partition $C = \{C_1, C_2, \ldots C_T\}$ of V into $T: = [N/k_0]$ clusters of size either $k_0$ or $k_0 + 1$.
2. **for** $n = 1, \ldots N$ **do**
   a. Let $C_t$ be the cluster to which vertex $v_n$ currently belongs.
   b. For each of the other clusters, $C_s$ such that $s \neq t$, compute the difference in information loss $\Delta_{n:t \to s}$, if $v_{n \text{ would}}$ move from $C_t$ to $C_s$.
   c. Let $C_{s0}$ be the cluster for which the loss $\Delta_{n:t \to s}$ is minimum.
   d. If $C_{t \text{ is}}$ singleton, move $v_n$ from $C_t$ to $C_{s0}$ and remove cluster $C_t$.
   e. else if $\Delta_{n:t \to s0} < 0$, move $v_n$ from $C_t$ to $C_{s0}$.
3. If there exist clusters of size greater than $k_1$, split each of them randomly into two equally-sized clusters.
4. If at least one vertex was moved during the last loop, then go to Step 2.
5. While there exist clusters of size smaller than k, select one of them and unify it with the cluster which is closest.
6. Output the resulting clusters.

The initial number of clusters is set to $T: = [N/k_0]$ and each one of their size is set to either $k_0$ or $k_0 + 1$, where $k_0 = \alpha k$ is an integer and $\alpha$ is a parameter that needs to be estimated. The main loop of the algorithm lies in steps 2-4 where it scans over N nodes in a cyclic manner and for each node, checks whether moving the node to another cluster decreases information loss. If such an improvement is possible, the transfer of node takes place to the best fitting cluster. In the main loop, the cluster size can vary between $[2, k_1]$, where $k_1 = \beta k$ for some predetermined fixed parameter $\beta$. When cluster size reduces to 1, we move the node to another best fitting cluster and delete the cluster. When the cluster size goes beyond $k_1$, we split it into two equally sized clusters in a random manner. The main loop runs either until there exists no node that can be transferred to another cluster while reducing information loss or until a suitable stopping criterion is met. In Goldberger and Tassa, (2010) Tassa et al. have run the main loop until improvement in information loss was less than a set threshold of 0.5% with the values of $\alpha$ and $\beta$ being 0.5 and 1.5 respectively. Once the main loop is completed and there exits clusters which are small, the agglomerative procedure in Step 5 takes care of these clusters. The closest cluster in Step 5 indicates that cluster which when combined with the target cluster causes smallest increase in information loss.

Parameters $\alpha$ and $\beta$ control the size of clusters. $\alpha$ has a smaller effect to information loss compared to $\beta$ because it is used only once in the beginning. If $\beta$ is too large or too small, we would have high information loss because large $\beta$ values give rise to large clusters and small $\beta$ values cause lot of small cluster to be unified in Step 5 leading to heavy information losses. Sequential clustering is known to have better performance in terms of runtime and quality compared to simulated annealing (Slonim, Friedman, & Tishby, 2002). Sequential clustering also performs better than SanGreeA algorithm which is a greedy algorithm introduced in (Campan & Truta, 2008). The reason why SanGreeA algorithm has low performance is because it does not have a mechanism to correct bad decisions that were made at an earlier stage. In terms of runtime, SanGreeA performs better requiring a complexity of $O(N^2)$ in evaluating the cost function while sequential clustering depends on $N^3$. This is because sequential clustering evaluates the information loss at each stage since at each stage it has a full clustering of all nodes. In Goldberger and Tassa (2010), a relaxed version of sequential clustering requiring $O(N^2)$ evaluations of the cost function by modifying the information loss measure and the sequential clustering algorithm has been implemented for centralized and distributed social networks as well.

## Clustering Algorithm Based on Distance-Preserving Subgraphs

Another interesting algorithm that can be used to achieve vertex clustering is the DP-Cluster algorithm proposed in Nussbaum, Esfahanian, and Tan (2010). This algorithm is based on partitioning a network into different distance-preserving clusters or subgraphs. A distance-preserving subgraph is a subgraph in which the shortest path between any two vertices in the subgraph is the same as the original graph. In Figure 1, the 4 clusters marked are all distance-preserving clusters. If any vertex is moved to from one cluster to another, then the 2 clusters no longer satisfy the distance-preserving property. Note that this algorithm works only for connected graphs and in case it should be applied to a disconnected graph, then the algorithm must be applied separately to all the components. We cannot test $2^n$ induced subgraphs to check if they are distance-preserving or not because it would require high computational capability. The best heuristic is to start with a single vertex as a cluster C which is trivially distance-preserving and at each step, an attempt is made to add a neighboring vertex not in C to C. If there is some non-empty set of neighboring vertices such that the union of a single element with C makes C distance-preserving, we choose one of them and permanently add it to C as per some predefined criteria. We stop when we reach a step where no neighboring vertices can be added to C while ensuring it remains distance-preserving. *Average distance increase* for a subgraph of G is defined as the distance between the subgraph and G, divided by the number of vertices in the subgraph. Therefore, distance-preserving subgraphs will have an average distance increase value of 0. Higher value of *average distance increase* indicates that the sub-graph is less distance-preserving.

The algorithm begins with each vertex in G as a cluster and one of these singleton clusters is chosen at random as the starting cluster. When there is more than one vertex to add to the current cluster, we chose a vertex at random. Once added, we set this vertex aside, pick another vertex at random, and repeat the process. Eventually, this will lead to G partitioned into some number of distance-preserving clusters. If cluster growth is not stopped at n=k vertices, we may end up with less that k distance-preserving clusters. When this happens, distance-preserving clusters are split to have k clusters. If we land up with more than k clusters, then clusters are merged in a manner where we can achieve most distance-preservation. In the algorithm, *clusters* is the set of clusters having members as vertices, *unused* is the set of vertices not yet placed in any cluster, *neighbors* is the set of available vertices which are adjacent to some vertex in the current cluster, *usable* is the set of vertices which can be added to the current cluster while ensuring the cluster remains distance-preserving. NEIGHBORS return the set of neighbors for a given vertex in a graph. RANDOMIZE returns a random permutation of a set. COUNT returns the number of elements in a set. ALMOST-DP returns how close a cluster is from being distance-preserving, measured using the *average distance increase* parameter. The pseudocode of the algorithm is given below:

**Input:** A graph G = (V, E) and an integer value k
**Output:** A partition of G into k disjoint clusters

1.  *unused* ← V
2.  **for** i ← 1 to n **do**

3.    $v \leftarrow$ RANDOM(*unused*)

4.    *unused* $\leftarrow$ *unused* / $\{v\}$

5.    *clusters*[i] $\leftarrow \{v\}$

6.    *neighbors* $\leftarrow$ NEIGHBORS (G, $v$) $\cap$ *unused*

7.    **while** unused **do**

8.    *neighbors* $\leftarrow$ RANDOMIZE(neighbors)

9.    *usable* $\leftarrow \{\}$

10.    **for** each $v \in$ *neighbors* **do**

11.    **if** IS_DP (G, *clusters*[i] $\cup$ $v$) **then**

12.    *usable* $\leftarrow$ *usable* $\cup$ $v$

13.    **end if**

14.    **end for**

15.    **if** *usable* $\neq \{\}$ **then**

16.    v $\leftarrow$ RANDOM(*usable*)

17.    *unused* $\leftarrow$ *unused* $\setminus \{v\}$

18.    *clusters*[i] $\leftarrow$ *clusters*[i] $\cup$ $v$

19.    *neighbors* $\leftarrow$ *neighbors* $\cup$ NEIGHBORS(G,v) $\cap$ *unused*

20.    **else**

21.    **break**

22.    **end if-else**

23.    **end while**

24.    $c_1, c_2 \leftarrow 0$

25.    *best* $\leftarrow \infty$

26.    **while** COUNT(*clusters*) > k **do**

27.    **for** each i $\in$ clusters **do**

28.    **for** each j $\in$ *clusters* $\setminus \{i\}$ **do**

29.    **if** ALMOST_DP(*clusters*, i, j) < *best* **then**

30.    $c_1 \leftarrow$ i

31.    $c_2 \leftarrow$ j

32.    *best* $\leftarrow$ ALMOST_DP(*clusters*, i, j)

33.    **end if**

34.    **end for**

35.    **end for**

36.    *clusters* $\leftarrow$ *clusters* $\cup$ $\{C_1 \cup C_2\} \setminus \{C_1, C_2\}$

37.    **end while**

38.    **end for**

39.    **return** *clusters*

The algorithm works in 2 parts. The first part is the heuristic which finds distance-preserving subgraphs and the second part is the metric used to merge subgraphs. Whenever the heuristic finds more than one neighbor vertex which can make the subgraph distance-preserving, random selection is used. Experiments have been performed on CiteSeer and Cora datasets using three tiebreaking parameters in clusters namely random, clustering coefficient and degree. Detailed experimental analysis of this approach can be found in in Nussbaum, Esfahanian, and Tan (2010).

## Clustering Algorithm Based on Vertex Connectivity

In Jiang, Xiong, and Zhang (2015), Huowen et al. proposed a clustering algorithm to achieve *k*-anonymity using vertex similarity. The similarity between vertices is defined using their connectivity by constructing a similarity matrix. Given a graph $G = (V, E)$ its similarity matrix is the square matrix $L(G) = (l_{i,j})_{nxn}$ where $l_{i,j}$ denotes the similarity between vertex i and vertex j.
If vertex i and vertex j are connected, then

$$\ell_{ij} = 1 - \frac{1}{\deg(v_i) + \deg(v_j) - 1}$$

If vertex I and vertex j are not connected, then

$$\ell_{ij} = \max_{P \subseteq P'} \left\{ \prod_{(v_s, v_t) \in P} \ell_{s,t} \right\},$$

where P' is the set of all shortest paths between $v_i$ and $v_j$ and P is the set of all vertex pairs on one of the shortest paths. When i=j, then $\ell_{ij}$ is zero. Higher the value of $\ell_{ij}$, greater is the probability that $v_i$ and $v_j$ will be partitioned into the same cluster. The distance between a vertex $v_i$ and cluster $C_j$ is given by,

$$dist(v_i, C_j) = \frac{|C_j|}{\sum_{\forall v_t \in C_j} \ell_{i,t}}$$

For any two clusters $C_i$ the probability that any of the two vertices in it are connected is given by the formula, $\dfrac{2\,|\,E_{C_i}\,|}{|\,C_i\,|\times(|\,C_i\,|-1)}$ where $|\,E_{C_i}\,|$ and $|\,C_i\,|$ are the number of edges and vertices in cluster $C_i$ respectively. The intra-cluster loss for $C_i$ is then defined by,

$$Inloss(C_i) = 2.\,|\,E_{C_i}\,|\,.\left(1 - \frac{2\,|\,E_{C_i}\,|}{|\,C_i\,|\times(|\,C_i\,|-1)}\right)$$

The inter-cluster loss between clusters $C_i$ and $C_j$ is given by,

$$btloss(C_i, C_j) = 2.\,|\,E_{C_i,C_j}\,|\,.\left(1 - \frac{|\,E_{C_i,C_j}\,|}{|\,C_i\,|\times|\,C_j\,|}\right)$$

Therefore the total loss is

$$iloss = \sum_{i=1}^{|V(G)|} inloss(C_i) + \sum_{i=1}^{|V(G)|}\sum_{j=1+1}^{|V(G)|} btloss(C_i, C_j)$$

The algorithm is called CBAC which is the short form for Clustering-based anonymization algorithm for social networks according to vertices connectivity. It constructs a cluster by first picking an un-clustered vertex randomly as the initial cluster and then keeps adding to it the remaining un-clustered vertices which have the shortest distance from the newly formed cluster. If more than one vertex has the same shortest distance to it, then they all go to it. The pseudo code of the algorithm is given below:

**Input:** A social network graph G, its adjacency matrix and anonymity parameter $k$.

**Output:** $k$-anonymized graph G*.

1.  V (G*) = Ø
2.  **while** |V(G)| > $k$
3.  $\forall v_r \in$ V(G)
4.  V(G) = V(G) − {$v_r$}
5.  C = {$v_r$}
6.  **while** |C| < $k$

7.   choose $v_t \in V(G)$ such that $dist(v_t, C) = \min\limits_{v_r \in V(G)} dist(v_r, C)$

8.   $V(G) = V(G) - \{v_t\}$

9.   $C = C \cup \{v_t\}$

10.  **end while**

11.  $V(G^*) = V(G^*) \cup \{C\}$

12.  **end while**

13.  **while** $|V(G)| \neq 0$

14.  $\forall v_r \in V(G)$

15.  $V(G) = V(G) - \{v_r\}$

16.  get $C_t \in V(G^*)$ such that $dist(v_r, C_t) = \min\limits_{C_s \in V(G^*)} dist(v_r, C_s)$

17.  $C_t = C_t \cup \{v_r\}$

18.  **end while**

19.  **for** every $C \in V(G^*)$, calculate $|C|$ and $|E_c|$, replacing C with ($|C|, |E_c|$)

20.  output $G^*$

In Jiang, Xiong, and Zhang (2015), Huowen et al. have compared the CBAC algorithm against the SASN algorithm proposed in Xiang (2013). CBAC has better time efficiency and lower information loss compared to SASN while varying $k$ from 2 to 6.

## EDGE CLUSTERING METHODS

This type of cluster-based anonymization involves aggregating edges on their type to prevent disclosure of sensitive relationships. Zheleva and Getoor (2007) considered a case where there are multiple types of edges but only one type of vertices. Among the various types of edges, one is considered to be a sensitive type which is to be hidden from the adversary. Therefore, for this particular scenario graph $G = (V, E)$ can be expressed as $G = (V, E_1, \ldots, E_k, E_s)$ where V is the set of vertices and $E_1, \ldots, E_k, E_s$ is the set of edges in the graph. An edge eij1 represents a relationship of type E1 between two vertices vi and vj. Es is the sensitive relationship and we must ensure that the edges belonging to this type must be undisclosed.

While anonymizing data, we may or may not release the sensitive relationships along with the released data. Sometimes even when sensitive relationships are not released, it may be possible to identify the sensitive relationships through observed relationships. Zheleva and Getoor (2007) focus on an adversary being able to predict sensitive edges based on observed edges. As a motivating example to this type of data model, we can consider in case in which vertices represent students and with three types of edges: classmates ($v_i$, $v_j$, c) [relationship between students vi and vj taking the same class c together], groupmates (vi, vj, g) [relationship between these students being in the same research group g] and friends (vi, vj) [ relationship of these students being friends which can be considered as a sensitive relationship]. Therefore, in this example our focus should be in understanding if friendship can be predicted based on class and research group rosters. The adversary is assumed to have a probabilistic model for predicting the sensitive edge based on a set of observations **O**: $P(e_{ij}^s|O)$. A noisy -or model (Pearl, 1988) has been assumed for the existence of the sensitive edge. According to the noisy -or model, the probability of a sensitive edge is:

$$P\ (e_{ij}^s = 1) = P\ (e_{ij}^s = 1\mid o_1, ..., o_n) = 1 - \prod_{l=0}^{n}\left(1 - \lambda l\right)$$

where $\lambda$ is the noise parameter and 'o' are the label observations based on the set of edges $e_{ij}$ . A noise parameter $\lambda_i$ captures the independent influence of an observed relationship $o_i$ on the existence of a sensitive relationship. In addition, there is also a leak parameter $\lambda_0$ which captures the probability that the sensitive edge is there due to another unmodeled reasons. The above formula applies only when the observations are certain. More details of the model can be found in Singliar and Hauskrecht (2006).

There were 5 edge anonymization methods proposed in Zheleva and Getoor (2007) which range from the one which has the lowest information loss to the one with the highest. The third and fourth anonymization techniques are cluster-edge anonymization approach but we have included the other 3 edge anonymization techniques as well for better understanding. These algorithms are to be applied to the network after the vertices have been anonymized using any technique such as k-anonymity using t-closeness which was introduced for single table data.

1. **Intact Edge Anonymization:** In this method, we simply remove the sensitive edges which keeping all other observational edges intact. In the motivating example discussed, this method would mean that we remove the sensitive friendship relationships and leave the information regarding

students taking common classes or being in the same research group untouched. Since relational observations are not disturbed, this technique has high utility of anonymized data but low privacy preservation. The output graph using this approach on a graph shown in Figure 4 (a) is given in Figure 4 (b). The pseudocode for this algorithm is given below:

a. **Input:** $G = (V, E^1, ..., E^s)$
b. **Output:** $G' = (V', E^{1'}, ..., E^{s'})$
c. $V' = $ anonymize-nodes $(V)$
d. **for** $t = 1$ to k **do**
e. $E^{t'} = E^t$
f. **end for**

2. **Partial-Edge Removal Anonymization:** In this technique, we remove some portion of the relational observations. Either a particular type of observation contributing to the overall likelihood of a sensitive relationship is removed or a certain percentage of observations meeting some pre-specified criteria (connecting high-degree vertices for example) is removed. This method increases privacy preservation but reduces the utility of data compared to intact edge technique. The output graph using this approach on Figure 4 (a) is given in Figure 5 (a). The pseudocode for this algorithm is given below:

a. **Input:** $G = (V, E^1, ..., E^k, E^s)$
b. **Output:** $G' = (V, E^{1'}, ..., E^{k'})$
c. $V' = $ anonymize-nodes $(V)$
d. **for** $t = 1$ to k **do**
e. $E^{t'} = E^t$
f. removed $ = $ percent $-$ removed $\times Et'$
g. **for** i=1 to removed **do**
h. $e_i = $ random edge from $E^{t'}$
i. $E^{t'} = E^{t'} \setminus \{ei\}$
j. **end for**
k. **end for**

3. **Cluster-Edge Anonymization:** In this approach, all the vertices of an equivalence class are collapsed into a single vertex and consider which edges are to be included in the collapsed graph. The simplest approach is to leave the sets of edges intact, and maintain a count of the number of edges between clusters of each edge type. The output graph using this approach on Figure 4 (a) is given in Figure 5 (b). The pseudocode of this algorithm is given below:

*Figure 4. The original graph (a) and intact edge anonymization (b)*

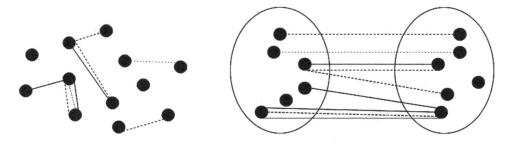

*Figure 5. Partial-edge removal anonymization (a) and cluster-edge anonymization (b)*

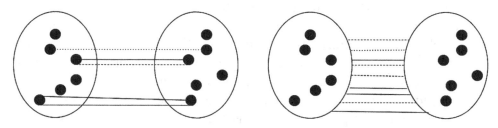

    a.    **Input:** $G = (V, E^1, ..., E^k, E^s)$
    b.    **Output:** $G' = (V, E^{1'}, ..., E^{k'})$
    c.    $V' = \{C_1, ..., C_m\}$
    d.    **for** t = 1 to k **do**
    e.    $E^{t'} = \varnothing$
    f.    **for** all $(v_i, vj) \in E^t$ **do**
    g.    $C_i = C(v_i)$
    h.    $C_j = C(vj)$
    i.    $E^{t'} = E^{t'} \cup \{(Ci, C_j)\}$
    j.    **end for**
    k.    **end for**

4.    **Cluster-Edge Anonymization With Constraints:** This is a stricter method for anonymization compared to the previous approach. We create edges between equivalence classes just as the previous method, but the equivalence class nodes should have the same constraints as any two nodes in the original data. For example, if the network has a constraint that there can be at most two edges of a certain type between entities, then there can be at most only two edges between the cluster nodes. This addition removes some of the count information that is revealed in the

previous technique. To determine the number of edges of a particular type connecting two equivalence classes, the anonymization algorithm picks the maximum of the number of edges of that type between any two nodes in the original graph. In our motivation example, if the maximum number of common classes that any pair of students from two equivalence class is one class together, then the equivalence classes are connected by one class edge. This methodology will keep some data utility but will not say anything of the distribution of observations. The output graph using this approach on Figure 4 (a) is given in Figure 6 (a). The pseudocode for this technique is given below:

a. **Input:** G= (V, E)
b. **Output:** G'= (V', E')
c. V' = {$C_1$,..., $C_m$}
d. **for** t = 1 to k **do**
e. $E^{t'}$ = Ø
f. **for** all ($v_i$, vj) ∈$E^t$ **do**
g. $C_i$ = C($v_i$)
h. $C_j$ = C(vj)
i. **if** (Ci $C_j$)} ∉ $E^{t'}$ **then**
j. $E^{t'}$ = $E^{t'}$ ∪ {(Ci $C_j$)}
k. **end if**
l. **end for**
m. 13.**end for**

5. **Removed Edges Anonymization:** This is the most conservation method where we remove all the edges. This technique is usually undesirable and it leads to low data utility and high privacy preservation. The output graph using this approach on Figure 4 (a) is given in Figure 6 (b). The pseudocode for this algorithm is given below:

*Figure 6. Cluster-edge anonymization with constraints (a) and removed edges anonymization (b)*

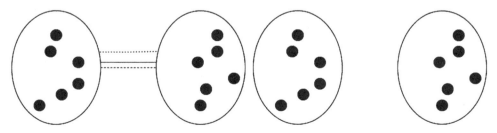

    a.   **Input:** G= (V, E)

    b.   **Output:** G'= (V', Ø)

    c.   V' = anonymize-nodes (V)

In Zheleva and Getoor (2007), the authors have run the algorithm for k values of 2 and 6 on dense and sparse graphs. At higher probability thresholds, keeping all the edges between equivalence classes preserves privacy better than deleting 50% of the two-node edges while simultaneously having high utility. Clustering-edge method gives low privacy preservation when k is low. With the clustering-edge method with constraints, both the values of k yielded same results. Cluster-edge method preserves privacy better in sparse graphs compared to dense graphs.

# GREEDY SEARCH METHODS FOR CLUSTERING SOCIAL NETWORKS

Generally, any algorithm which makes a locally optimum decision in the hope that this choice will eventually lead to the global minimum. It always takes the decision that seems to be the best decision at the moment. Once a particular decision is taken, the greedy algorithm never goes back to change its decision. Using these algorithms as the main anonymization procedure certain clustering algorithms having been developed for anonymizing social networks.

## saNGreeA Algorithm

Social Network Greedy Anonymization (saNGreeA) is an algorithm that uses a greedy clustering technique to generate a k-anonymized generalized social network. The algorithm is evaluated on two types of losses namely generalization information loss and the structural information loss. Generalization information Loss (GIL) is the loss due to generalization of quasi-identifier attributes in the graph and Structural Information Loss (SIL) is a measure of the loss in structural information while anonymizing a graph through collapsing clusters into nodes, together with their neighborhoods. Inter-cluster and Intra-cluster structural information losses have been considered. NGIL refers to normalized GIL. In-depth details about these losses can be found in Campan and Truta (2008).

The anonymization algorithm combines vertices that are as similar as possible, both in terms of their quasi-identifier attribute values, and in terms of their neighborhood structure so that the GIL and SIL are low. Suppose G = (V, E) is a graph with vertices in a particular order $\{X^1, X^2, \ldots\ldots X^n\}$ then the neighborhood of a vertex $X^i$ is represented by a Boolean vector $Bi = (b_1^i, b_2^i, \ldots\ldots b_n^i)$ where the jth component $b_j^i$ is 1 if there is an edge $(X^i, X^j) \in$ E and 0 otherwise provided $j \neq i$. $b_i^i$ is considered to be undefined therefore not equal to 1 or 0. Distance between two vertices $X^i$ and $X^j$ is given by the formula:

$$dist(X^i, X^j) = \frac{\left|\{l \mid l = 1\ldots n \wedge l \neq i, j; b_l^i \neq b_{l^j}\}\right|}{n - 2}$$

The denominator is divided by n-2 because i and j components that are equal to each other are undefined and hence ignored. To measure the structural distance between a vertex X and a cluster $cl$ the we use the following formula:

$$dist(X, cl) = \frac{\sum\limits_{X^j \in cl} dist(X, X^j)}{|cl|}$$

Both distance measures take values between 0 and 1. We input parameters $\alpha$ and $\beta$ whose main purpose is to control the relative importance given to the total generalization information loss and the total structural information loss. Their sum $[\alpha + \beta]$ has to be 1. The pseudocode for the sanGreeA algorithm is given below:

**Input:** G = (V, E) – a social network, integer value $k$ and user defined weight parameters – $\alpha$, $\beta$.

**Output:** Anonymized network S = $\{cl_1, cl_2, \ldots cl_v\}$ where $\bigcup\limits_{j=1}^{v} cl_j = V$ and $|cl| > k$ for every cluster and no two clusters have the same vertex.

1.  S = $\emptyset$; i =1
2.  **Repeat**
3.  $X^{seed}$ = a node with maximum degree from V
4.  $cl_i = \{ X^{seed} \}$
5.  V = V - $\{ X^{seed} \}$

6.  **Repeat**
7.  X* =

// X* is the vertex with V (Unselected nodes) that produces the minimal information loss growth when added to $cl_i$ .
//$G_1$ – the subgraph introduced by cl $\cup$ {X} in G
//$S_1$ – the partition with one cluster cl $\cup$ {X}

8.  $cl_i = cl_i \cup \{ X^* \}$ ; V = V – { X* }
9.  **Until** ($cl_i$ has *k* elements) or (V == $\varnothing$)
10.  **if** ($|cl_i| \leq$ k) **then**
11.  DisperseCluster(S, $cl_i$); // happens only for the last cluster
12.  **else**
13.  S = S $\cup$ $\{cl_i\}$; i++
14.  **end** if
15.  **Until** N = $\varnothing$
16.  **End** GreedyPKClustering.
17.  **Function** DisperseCluster(S, cl)
18.  **for** every X $\in$ cl **do**
19.  $cl_u$ = FindBestCluster(X, S)
20.  $cl_u = cl_u \cup \{X\}$
21.  **end** for
22.  **end** DisperseCluster
23.  **Function** FindBestCluster(X, S)
24.  bestCluster = null; infoLoss = $\infty$
25.  **for** every $cl_j \in$ S **do**
26.  **if** $\alpha \bullet$ NGIL(G1, S1) + $\beta \bullet$ dist(X, $cl_j$)<infoLoss **then**
27.  infoLoss = $\alpha \bullet$ NGIL(G1, S1) + $\beta \bullet$ dist(X, $cl$j)
28.  bestCluster = $cl_j$
29.  **end** if
30.  **end** for
31.  return bestCluster;
32.  **end** FindBestCluster

To form a new cluster, a vertex V with the maximum degree and not yet allocated to any cluster is selected as a seed for the new cluster. The algorithm then gathers nodes to this currently processed cluster until it reaches the desired cardinality *k*. At each step, the current cluster grows with one node and the selected node has to be unallocated yet to any cluster and to minimize the cluster's information loss growth which is quantified as a weighted measure that combines NGIL and *dist*. When the total number of nodes is not a multiple of k then there is a possibility that the last cluster would contain less than *k* nodes. In that case, each of this cluster's vertices will be added to the cluster whose information loss will minimally increase by that node addition. This is the main role of the function DisperseCluster. Campan and Truta have run the algorithm on a random graph and the R_MAT graph model. They have considered α, β values of (0.0, 1.0) which guides the algorithm towards minimizing the structural information loss, without giving any consideration to the generalization information loss factor and (0.5, 0.5) which equally weights both the information loss components. Information Loss used in saNGreeA is IL = α. NGIL(G, S) + β.D(*v,cl*) where NGIL is the normalized general information loss and D(*v,cl*) is the distance between a vertex *v* and cluster *cl* whose formulas can be found in Wang, Zhang, Feng, and Fu (2015). The results of their experiments can be inferred from Campan and Truta (2008).

saNGreeA algorithm protects the quasi-identifier attributes and structure information from re-identification attacks without having any restriction on the sensitive attributes. Consider an unmasked graph given in Figure 7 and its attributes given in Table 1.

saNGreeA algorithm will then generate a *k*-anonymous masked network as given in Figure 8 along with its generalized attributes in Table 2.

*Figure 7. An unmasked social network graph*

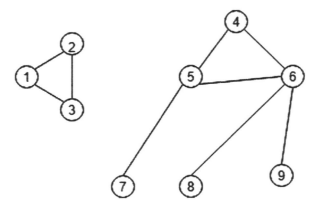

*Table 1. Attributes of an unmasked social network graph*

| Node | Age | Zip | Gender | Disease |
|------|-----|-----|--------|---------|
| 1 | 15 | 41070 | M | Cancer |
| 2 | 17 | 41005 | M | Cancer |
| 3 | 12 | 41035 | M | Cancer |
| 4 | 67 | 45032 | F | Malaria |
| 5 | 54 | 40001 | M | AIDS |
| 6 | 21 | 42073 | F | Dengue |
| 7 | 45 | 41022 | F | AIDS |
| 8 | 33 | 41078 | M | Dengue |
| 9 | 27 | 41066 | F | Dengue |

*Figure 8. A k-anonymous masked social network graph generated by saNGreeA algorithm*

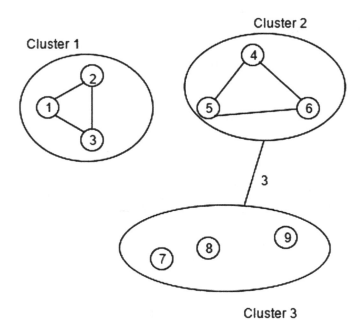

*Table 2. Attributes of k-anonymous masked social network graph generated by saNGreeA algorithm*

| Node | Age | Zip | Gender | Disease |
|------|-----|-----|--------|---------|
| 1 | 12-17 | 410** | M | Cancer |
| 2 | 12-17 | 410** | M | Cancer |
| 3 | 12-17 | 410** | M | Cancer |
| 4 | 21-67 | ***** | * | Malaria |
| 5 | 21-67 | ***** | * | AIDS |
| 6 | 21-67 | ***** | * | Dengue |
| 7 | 27-45 | 410** | * | AIDS |
| 8 | 27-45 | 410** | * | Dengue |
| 9 | 27-45 | 410** | * | Dengue |

# Extension of saNGreeA Algorithm to Account for *l* -Diversity

saNGreeA algorithm could generate a k-anonymous Masked Social Network (MSN) with respect to both quasi-identifier attributes and relations given an initial social network SN (V, E). MSN is defined as a triple Masked Graph MG (*MV, ME, MA*), where:

- Masked Vertices $(MV) = \{cl_1, cl_2, \ldots, cl_m\}$ is a partition of the vertices of *SN*, containing *m* clusters, generated by SaNGreeA where each cluster contains at least *k* vertices, $cl_i \cap cl_j = \emptyset (i \neq j)$, and $\bigcup_{i=1}^{m} cl_i = V$.
- Masked Edges *(ME)* is the set of the edges between the clusters: $(cl_i, cl_j) \in ME(i \neq j)$, if there exists a $v_p \in cl_i$ *and* $v_q \in cl_j$, such that $(v_p, v_q) \in E$.
- Masked Attributes *(MA)* is the set of corresponding tuples of the clusters' vertices, including sensitive attributes and generalized quasi-identifier attributes.

An extended version of this algorithm to provide $l$-diversity anonymization as well was proposed by Wang et al. (2015). Their algorithm called MASN can produce a Further Masked Social Network [FMSN] that can fulfill both $k$-anonymity and $l$-diversity. FMSN is defined as Further Masked Graph FMG (*FMV, FME, FMA*), where:

- Further Masked Vertices (*FMV*) = *{cl$_1$', cl$_2$', ……, cl$_m$'}* is a partition of the vertices of *SN*, containing $n$ clusters, generated by MASN where each cluster contains at least $k$ vertices, $cl_i' \cap cl_j' = \emptyset (i \neq j)$, and $\bigcup_{i=1}^{n} cl_i'$ = V.
- Further Masked Edges (*FME*) is the set of the edges between the clusters: $(cl_i', cl_j') \in FME(i \neq j)$, if there exists a $v_p \in cl_i'$ and $v_q \in cl_j'$, such that $(v_p, v_q) \in E$ .
- Further Masked Attributes (*FMA*) is the set of corresponding tuples of the clusters' vertices, including sensitive attributes and generalized quasi-identifier attributes. Each cluster has at-least $l$ distinct sensitive attributes.

It can be observed from Figure 8 and Table 2 that saNGreeA algorithm is susceptible if an adversary is able to use background information to know the age of his target. If his target is a teenager, then it can be inferred that the target has Cancer. To combat this problem, we add $l$- diversity criterion. The main algorithm is called MASN which uses two other algorithms FindBestCl and Disperse. In MASN, *Div*(cl) is the diversity of cluster cl. Information loss used in this approach is IL' = $\alpha$. NGIL(G, S) + $\beta$.NSIL(G, S) where S is the partitioning of G into clusters S = {cl$_1$,….,cl$_n$}, NGIL is the normalized general information loss and NSIL is the normalized structural information loss. The pseudocode of the algorithms is given below:

## Algorithm: MASN

**Input:** G = (V, E) – a social network, integer values $k$ *and* $l$, user defined weight parameters – $\alpha$, $\beta$ where $\alpha + \beta = 1$

**Output:** Further Masked Graph *FMG*(*FMV, FME, FMA*) which satisfies k-anonymity and $l$ - diversity .

1. *MG*(*MV, ME, MA*) $\leftarrow$ *SaNGreeA*(*G, k, $\alpha$, $\beta$*);
2. *FMV* $\leftarrow$ *{cl\|cl $\in$ MV,* and *cl* satisfies $l$ -diversity*}*;

3.  $NFMV \leftarrow MV - FMV$ [$NFMV$ has all those clusters that don't satisfy $l$ -diversity ]
4.  **while** $NFMV \neq \varnothing$
5.  get $cl_{e1} \in NFMV$, such that for all $cl \in NFMV$ $(cl \neq cl_{e1})$ and $Div(cl_{e1}) \geq Div(cl)$
6.  $NFMV \leftarrow NFMV - \{cl_{e1}\};$
7.  **while** $Div(cl_{e1}) < l$
8.  $(cle2, ve1, ve2) \leftarrow FindBestCl(cl_{e1}, FMV, NFMV)$
9.  **if** $cle2 \neq \varnothing$ **then**
10. Swap $ve1$ with $ve2$
11. **else**
12. $Disperse(cl_{e1}, FMV, NFMV)$ and **goto** STEP 4;
13. **end** if-else
14. **end** while
15. $FMV \leftarrow FMV \cup \{cl_{e1}\} \cup \{cl|cl \in NFMV, Div(cl) \geq l \}$
16. $NFMV \leftarrow NFMV - \{cl|cl \in NFMV, Div(cl) \geq l \}$
17. **end** while
18. Generate $FME$ and $FMA$ according to $FMV$
17. **return** $FMG$

## Algorithm: FindBestCl

$FMV$ is a set whose elements are clusters that satisfy $l$ -diversity;
    $NFMV$ is a set whose elements are clusters that don't satisfy $l$ -diversity
    **Input:** A cluster $cl_{e1}$; FMV, NFMV
    **Output:** $(cl_{e2}, v_{e1}, v_{e2})$, where $cl_{e2}$ is a cluster, $v_{e1} \in cl_{e1}$, and $v_{e2} \in cl_{e2}$;

1.  $V_e \leftarrow \{v|v \in cl,$ where $cl \in FMV \cup NFMV\}$
2.  $VP \leftarrow cl_{e1} \times V_e$
3.  $(cl_{e2}, v_{e1}, v_{e2}) \leftarrow (\varnothing, NULL, NULL)$
4.  **while** $VP \neq \varnothing$ and $cl_{e2} = \varnothing$
5.  $(v_1{}^*, v_2{}^*) \leftarrow \underset{(v_1, v_2) \in VP}{\arg \min} (IL'{}^* (G, FMV \cup NFMV \cup \{cl_{e1}\}))$

    // IL'* is the information loss after swapping $v1$ with $v2$.

6.  **if** $Div (cl_{e1} \cup \{v_2{}^*\} - \{v_1{}^*\}) \leq Div(cl_{e1})$ **then**
7.  $VP \leftarrow VP - \{(v_1{}^*, v_2{}^*)\}$
8.  **else if** $v_2{}^* \in cl$ $(cl \in FMV)$ **and** $Div(cl \cup \{v_1{}^*\} - \{v_2{}^*\}) < l$ **then**

9. $VP \leftarrow VP - \{(v_1{}^*, v_2{}^*)\}$
10. **else**
11. $v_{e1} \leftarrow v_1{}^*, v_{e2} \leftarrow v_2$
12. $cl_{e2} \leftarrow cl(v_{e2} \in cl)$
13. **end** if-else
14. **end** while
15. **return** $(cl_{e2}, v_{e1}, v_{e2})$

## Algorithm: Disperse

**Input:** A cluster $cl_{e1}$, FMV, NFMV

1. **for** each $v$ in $cl_{e1}$
2. $cl* \leftarrow \underset{cl \in FMV \cup NFMV}{\arg\min} (IL'* (G, FMV \cup NFMV))$

   \\ IL'* is the information loss after moving $v$ into cl.

3. $cl* \leftarrow cl* \cup \{v\}$
4. $cl_{e1} \leftarrow cl_{e1} - \{v\};$

MASN increases the diversity ($Div()$) of a cluster $cl_{e1}$ that doesn't satisfy $l$-diversity through vertex-swapping, which fulfills the following requirements after swapping:

- $Div(cl_{e1})$ increases;
- Clusters in FMV are still here;
- The information loss is minimal.

The $k$-anonymous, $l$ – diversity masked graph generated by MASN using Figure 7 as input is given in Figure 9 and its generalized attributes in Table 3. Experiments conducted in Wang et al. (2015) show that MASN can achieve higher security than saNGreeA with almost the same utility.

## CLUSTERING DYNAMIC SOCIAL NETWORKS

Real social networks usually evolve with time so it is important to understand how clustering techniques can be applied to them. A dynamic social network is an initial graph G plus an infinite change stream $c_1, \ldots, c_\infty$ where each

*Figure 9. A k-anonymous, l – diversity masked social network graph generated by MASN algorithm*

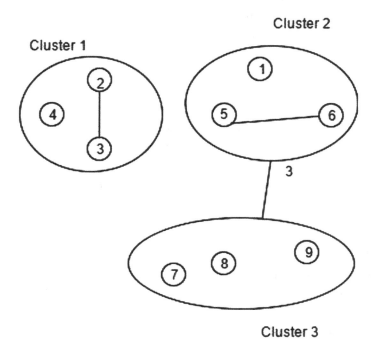

*Table 3. Attributes of A k-anonymous, l – diversity masked social network graph generated by MASN algorithm*

| Node | Age | Zip | Gender | Disease |
|------|-------|--------|--------|---------|
| 4 | 12-67 | 410** | M | Malaria |
| 2 | 12-67 | 410** | M | Cancer |
| 3 | 12-67 | 410** | M | Cancer |
| 1 | 15-54 | ***** | * | Cancer |
| 5 | 15-54 | ***** | * | AIDS |
| 6 | 15-54 | ***** | * | Dengue |
| 7 | 27-45 | 410** | * | AIDS |
| 8 | 27-45 | 410** | * | Dengue |
| 9 | 27-45 | 410** | * | Dengue |

change $c_i$ can either be an edge deletion, vertex addition, edge addition, vertex deletion which are denoted as *uv-*, *u+*, *uv+*, *u-* respectively. In this section, we will look at one particularly interesting incremental clustering approach that clusters a dynamic social network into *k*-cliques.

## Incremental *k*-Clique Clustering

Incremental clustering processes vertices one at a time. A $k$ – clique is a complete subgraph with $k$ vertices. Note that a clique is a complete subgraph so every two vertices in a clique are joined by an edge in the original graph. Two $k$ -cliques are adjacent to each other if they have $k - 1$ common nodes. *k*- clique clustering is a union of all *k*-cliques that can be reached from each other through a series of adjacent *k*-cliques. In Figure 10, we can observe what a 3-clique looks like and the 3-clique clusters of a toy example. Suppose P is the *k*-clique clusters of graph G, then incremental *k*-clique clustering in dynamic social networks involves locally updating P such that when a change c in the change stream happens, it is the right k-clique clusters of the changed network G' = G + c.

## Incremental 2-Clique Clustering

We shall look at the case when $k = 2$ in this chapter. 2-clique clusters are the connected components of the graph that can be solved by depth first search (DFS). The clustering result can be expressed by a DFS forest F in which nodes from the same DFS tree form a cluster. Therefore, the main part of

*Figure 10. 3-clique and 3-clique clusters of a network*

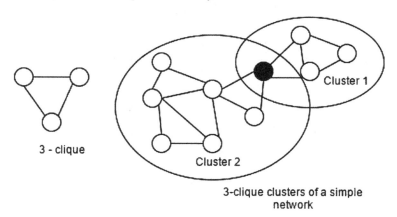

3 - clique

Cluster 1

Cluster 2

3-clique clusters of a simple network

2-clique clustering is to obtain DFS forest F of graph G and incremental 2-clique clustering is converted to local DFS forest updating depending on a given change $c$. This algorithm was proposed by Duan et al. (2012). The algorithm for updating a local DFS forest is given below:

*Algorithm: Local DFS Forest Updating*

**Input:** graph G, DFS forest F and change c
   **Output:** updated G and F

1.   **if** type of c is edge deletion **then**
2.   call TED(G, F, $c.u$, $c.v$)
3.   **if** type of c is node deletion **then**
4.   **for** all neighbors $u$ of $c.v$ in G **do**
5.   call TED(G, F, u, $c.v$)
6.   delete node $c.v$ from G and F
7.   **if** type of c is edge addition **then**
8.   call TEA(G, F, $c.u$, $c.v$)
9.   **if** type of c is node addition **then**
10.  add node $c.v$ into G and F
11.  return updated G and F

Local DFS Forest updating depends on two other algorithms TED (Two-clique Edge Deletion) and TEA (Two-clique Edge Addition). Before reading on these algorithms, note that edges are classified into two types namely forward and backward. Forward edges are those edges present in DFS forest F and backward edges are those not present in the DFS forest F but in graph G.

## Two-Clique Edge Deletion (TED)

If we need to delete a backward edge, then we simply delete it from G and keep F unchanged because backward edges are not present in F. If we need to delete a forward edge, then a couple of steps must be followed. Suppose the edge to be delete is the edge $uv$ in Figure 11 (a) where $u$ is the parent of $v$ and subtree[$v$] is the subtree rooted at $v$, then deleting edge $uv$ will make subtree[$v$] detached from the tree. However, we can connect it back to the tree if backward edges are present. We can choose the nearest backward edge legally but we need to ensure that two vertices adjacent to a backward edge satisfy ancestor-descendant relation. In Figure 11 (a), we can reconnect wither subtree[*v*] via backward edge e$_1$ or e$_2$. Connecting through e$_1$ will violate the ancestor-descendant relation for the adjacent vertices of e$_2$ which can be observed in Figure 11 (b). Therefore, we connect via e$_2$ to ancestor as shown in Figure 11 (c). The selected ancestor is denoted as,

$$alt[v] = \begin{cases} \arg\max\limits_{u \in cand[v]} order \; [u] & if \; cand[v] \neq \phi \\ v & otherwise \end{cases}$$

where cand[*v*] is the candidate set of ancestors of v connecting to subtree[v] through backward edges, order [*u*] is the DFS order of node *u*. If *alt[v] =* *v*, then *subtree[v]* is really detached from the DFS tree when we delete *uv* because *uv* is the only edge connecting *subtree[v]* to the tree. In this case, *subtree[v]* is cut from the original tree and it is added to forest F as a new DFS tree. In practical applications, this kind of edge deletion splits a large cluster into two small ones. If *alt[v] ≠ v*, there are ancestors of *v* connected to *subtree[v]* via backward edges. In this case, *subtree[v]* is not truly detached from the original tree since there exist backward edges through which we can re-connect *subtree[v]*. One of these backward edges will be between *alt[v]* and some node in subtree[v]. However, the deletion of uv might cause the DFS order of vertices in S = {*alt[v]*} ∪ {*w*|*w* ∈ *subtree[v]*} to change. To sum up, DFS must be re-performed on subgraph G(S) starting from node *alt[v]*. After DFS on G(S), the resultant DFS tree is connected to the original DFS tree in the position of node alt[v]. The pseudo code for this algorithm is given below

## Algorithm: TED

**Input:** graph G, forest F and node *u* and *v*
    **Output:** updated G and F

1.    delete *uv* from G
2.    **if** *uv* is a forward edge **then**
3.    **if** *alt[v] = v* **then**
4.    detach *subtree[v]* from *tree[v]*
5.    add *subtree[v]* to F
6.    **else**
7.    S ← { *alt[v]*} ∪ {*w*| *w*∈*subtree[v]* }

8.   t ← DFS(G(S))
9.   **for** all child *cld* of *root(t)* **do**
10.  connect *cld* to *alt[v]* as a child tree
11.  **end if - else**
12.  **end if**
13.  **return** updated G and F

The best time complexity when we delete a forward edge is O(log N) and the worst case is O(log N + $\left|subtree\left[v\right]\right|$).

## Two-Clique Edge Addition (TEA)

There are three possible types of edges that can be added to a graph: backward edge (Type 1), edge between two nodes that violate the ancestor-descendant relation in the same DFS tree (Type 2) and an edge crossing two DFS trees. Addition of type 1 edge is simple and direct because backward edges do not change the DFS tree. When we need to add an edge of type 2, the DFS order of the tree is highly likely to change. Consider Figure 12, suppose the edge to be added is *uv*+ then X is the nearest common ancestor of *u* and *v*. After adding an edge between *u* and *v*, the child tree of X (indicated by subgraph G

*Figure 11. (a) original DFS tree of a network (b) DFS tree after uv- and connecting subtree[v] through backward edge e₁ (c) DFS tree after after uv- and connecting subtree[v] through backward edge e₂*

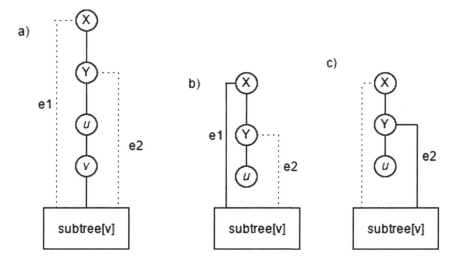

*Figure 12. Type-2 edge addition in TEA*

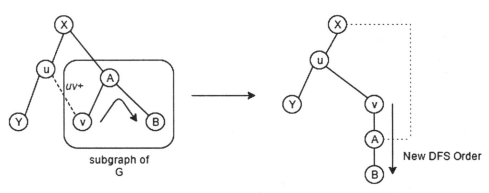

in Figure 12) can be directly reached through vertex *u* during DFS. Therefore, we reperform DFS on subgraph G (the resultant direction is indicated by an arrow in subgraph G) and we connect this new DFS tree to node *u*. After this procedure, edge between X and A is no longer in the DFS tree and is considered to be a backward edge.

Let us now consider the case where we need to add an edge of type 3. Suppose we have two DFS trees from graphs g($t$) and g($r$) called tree $t$ (*tree[u]*) and tree $r$ (*tree[v]*) and we need to add an edge between nodes *u* and *v* (see Figure 13), we perform DFS on graph g(r) starting from node *v* and connect the resultant DFS tree to node *u*. Note that here we connected tree *r* to tree *t* but we could have connected tree *t* to tree *r* instead as well since the edges are symmetric. In practice, the smaller DFS tree is connected to the larger tree to reduce the size of graph requiring DFS.

The pseudo code for TEA algorithm is given below

*Figure 13. Type-3 edge addition in TEA*

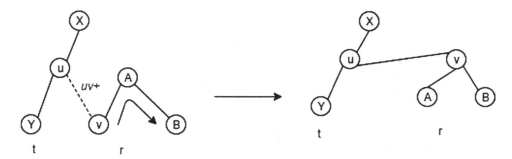

## Algorithm: TEA

**Input:** graph G, forest F, nodes *u* and *v*
   **Output:** updated G and F

1.   add *uv* into G
2.   **if** *tree[u]=tree[v]* **then**
3.   *w* ←nearest common ancestor of *u* and *v*
4.   **if** $w \neq u$ and $w \neq v$ **then**
5.   *t* ← *w*'s child tree that contains *v*
6.   detach *t* from *tree[u]*
7.   R ← {*x*|*x* ∈ *t*}
8.   DFS on G(R) starting at node v
9.   connect the new DFS tree to node u
10.  **end if**
11.  **else**
12.  *t* ← *tree[v]*
13.  R ← {*x*|*x* ∈ *t*}
14.  remove *t* from F
15.  DFS on G(R) starting at node *v*
16.  connect the new DFS tree to node *u*
17.  **end if-else**
18.  **return** updated G and F

The best time complexity of edge addition is O(1) and the worst is O($\left|tree\left[v\right]\right|$) . Overall, the best complexity of DFS forest updating is O(1) and the worst is O(max(log N + $\left|subtree\left[v\right]\right|$, $\left|tree\left[v\right]\right|$)). General incremental *k*-clique clustering (case when $k \geq 3$) can be referred from Duan et al. (2012).

## REFERENCES

Campan, A., & Truta, T. M. (2008). Data and Structural k-Anonymity in Social Networks. *Proceedings from the Second ACM SIGKDD International Workshop on Privacy, Security, and Trust in KDD (PinKDD)*, 33-54.

Chakrabarti, D., Zhan, Y., & Faloutsos, C. (2004). R-MAT: A Recursive Model for Graph Mining. *SIAM International Conference on Data Mining.* doi:10.1137/1.9781611972740.43

Cormode, G., Srivastava, D., Bhagat, S., & Krishnamurthy, B. (2009). Classbased graph anonymization for social network data. *Proc. Very Large Data Bases Endowment, 2*(1), 766–777.

Duan, D., Li, Y., Li, R., & Lu, Z. (2012). Incremental K-clique clustering in dynamic social networks. *Artificial Intelligence Review, 38*(2), 129–147. doi:10.1007/s10462-011-9250-x

Goldberger, J., & Tassa, T. (2010). Efficient Anonymizations with Enhanced Utility. *Transactions on Data Privacy, 3*, 149–175.

Hay, M., Miklau, G., Jensen, D., Towsley, D., & Weis, P. (2010). Resisting structural re-identification in anonymized social networks. *The Very Large Database BasesJournal, 19*(6), 797–823. doi:10.1007/s00778-010-0210-x

Jiang, H., Xiong, H., & Zhang, H. (2015). A novel approach to achieving k-anonymization for social network privacy preservation based on vertex connectivity. *Proceedings of the Advanced Information Technology, Electronic, and Automation Control Conference (IAEAC).*

Liu, K., & Terzi, E. (2008). Towards identity anonymization on graphs. In *Proceedings of the ACM SIGMOD International Conference on Management of Data* (pp. 93–106). New York: ACM Press.

Nussbaum, R., Esfahanian, A. H., & Tan, P. N. (2010). Clustering social networks using distance-preserving subgraphs. *Proceedings of the 2010 International Conference on Advances in Social Networks Analysis and Mining (ASONAM), 380–385.* doi:10.1109/ASONAM.2010.78

Pearl, J. (1988). *Probabilistic Reasoning in Intelligent Systems: Networks of Plausible Inference.* San Mateo, CA: Morgan Kaufmann Publishers, Inc.

Russell, S. J., & Norvig, P. (2003). *Artificial Intelligence: A Modern Approach.* Pearson Education Limited.

Singliar, T., & Hauskrecht, M. (2006). Noisy-or component analysis and its application to link analysis. *Journal of Machine Learning Research, 7,* 2189–2213.

Slonim, N., Friedman, N., & Tishby, N. (2002). Unsupervised Document Classification Using Sequential Information Maximization. *Proceedings on 25th Annual International ACM SIGIR Conference on Research and Development in Information Retrieval (SIGIR)*, 129-136. doi:10.1145/564376.564401

Tassa, T., & Cohen, D. (2013). Anonymization of Centralized and Distributed Social Networks by Sequential Clustering. *IEEE Transactions on Knowledge and Data Engineering, 25*(2), 311-324.

Wang, R., Zhang, M., Feng, D., & Fu, Y. (2015). A Clustering Approach for Privacy-Preserving in Social Networks. In J. Lee & J. Kim (Eds.), Lecture Notes in Computer Science: Vol. 8949. *Information Security and Cryptology - ICISC 2014. ICISC 2014*. Cham: Springer. doi:10.1007/978-3-319-15943-0_12

Xiang, K. L. (2013). *Research on Privacy preserving in social networking based on graph modification and clustering* (Master's dissertation). Zhejiang University.

Zheleva, E., & Getoor, L. (2007). Preserving the privacy of sensitive relationships in graph data. *Proceedings of the 1st ACM SIGKDD Workshop on Privacy, Security, and Trust in KDD (PinKDD'07)*.

# Chapter 5
# Graph Modification Approaches

## ABSTRACT

*This chapter contains some of the most recent techniques and algorithms on social network anonymisation. The authors start with the random perturbation algorithms like the UMGA algorithm and constrained perturbation algorithms like the fast k-degree anonymization (FKDA) algorithm. Then they move to the anonymisation technique, noise nodes addition, and present an algorithm based upon this approach. Next, the authors move on to α-anonymization, (α, k) anonymity, (α, l) diversity, and recursive (α, c, l) diversity anonymisation algorithms, which are generalisations in that order.*

## INTRODUCTION

Clustering methods provide suitable privacy measures but the analysis of local measures and metrics from the anonymized graphs are not straightforward. In addition, the anonymized graph is generally shrunk considerably and may be undesirable for analyzing local structures. Graph modification based anonymization methods alter number of vertices or edges in the graph. To preserve the size and local structures of the graph, these approaches try to locally modify the graph structure to provide privacy protection.

DOI: 10.4018/978-1-5225-5158-4.ch005

# RANDOM PERTURBATION

These methods involve adding random noise to the data. They protect against re-identification in a probabilistic manner. In this section, we will look at an algorithm called the UMGA Algorithm.

## UMGA Algorithm

UMGA algorithm was proposed by Casas-Roma et al. (2016). The algorithm aims to construct a $k$ – degree anonymous network using minimum number of edge modifications and the vertices are left unchanged. Given a graph G = (V, E), $v_i \in$ V refers to vertex $i$ and { $v_i, v_j$ } refers to the undirected edge between vertices $i$ and $j$. $n$ is the number of vertices and $m$ us the number of edges in the graph G. $d$ is the degree sequence of G having a length of $n$. An ordered degree sequence has a monotonic non-decreasing sequence of vertex degrees such that $d_i \leq d_j$ for all $i$ less than $j$. The average degree of G is denoted by $<deg>$ which is equal to ($2m/n$). Note that we use $2m$ to calculate the average degree because we consider only undirected graphs, so each edge is counted twice. The set of one neighborhood of vertex $v_i$ is denoted as $\Gamma(v_i)$. The algorithm first constructs a $k$-degree anonymous sequence $\tilde{d} = \{ \tilde{d}_1,...,\tilde{d}_n \}$ from the degree sequence $d$ and then modifies the network to have the anonymous degree sequence through edge modifications. Function $\Delta$ is used to measure the distance between $\tilde{d}$ and $d$.

$$\Delta = \sum_{i=1}^{n} \left| \tilde{d}_i - d_i \right|$$

Therefore, low value of $\Delta$ indicates low information loss in the anonymized network. To make $d$ $k$-anonymous we must group it into groups of $k$ or more elements. Optimal univariate micro-aggregation (Hansen & Mukherjee, 2003) is used to achieve this task. Aggregation is just another name for clustering and in micro-aggregation, to protect privacy, instead of releasing sensitive values for individual records, records are aggregated into groups and the mean of the group to which an observation belongs is released. $d$ is assumed to be an ordered degree sequence of the original network. If not, a permutation *f* to the sequence to reorder the elements. Initially, a new directed network $H_{k,n}$ is created according to Hansen & Mukherjee (2003).

## Directed Network $H_{k,n}$ Generation

We input a vector length of *n* which can be the vertices vector or the degree vector sorted in ascending order followed by the value of *k*. Let's call the vector V. For each element $v_i$ in V (*i* ranging from 1 to *k*), the network has a vertex with label *i*. The graph also has an additional vertex with label 0. For each pair of graph nodes $(i, j)$ such that $i + k \leq j < i + 2k$, the graph has a directed arc $(i, j)$ from vertex *i* to vertex *j*. For each arc $(i, j)$, the corresponding group $C_{(i,j)}$ is the set of values $\{v_h : i < h \leq j\}$.

After generating the directed network, it's optimal partition is computed which is exactly the set of groups that correspond to the arcs of the shortest path from vertex 0 to vertex *n* in $H_{k,n}$. This optimal partition is denoted by $g = \{g_1, ..., g_p\}$ where p ranges anywhere from $(n/k)$ to $(n/2k-1)$ and each $g_i$ has between *k* and 2*k*-1 items. Every element $d_i \in d$ belongs to a group in *g*. After optimal partition, a matrix of differences denoted by $M_{p\times2}$ using each group in the partition. The columns are the sum of differences between each element of the group and the arithmetic mean of all degrees that belong to the group. The first column is computed using the floor function to get the number of degrees we should decrease in the group to get *k*-anonymity. These values are always zero or positive. The second column is computed using the ceil function to get the number of degrees we should increase in the group to get *k*-anonymity. These values are always negative or zero. For $j = \{1, ..., p\}$ each element $m_{ji}$ of the matrix $M_{p\times2}$ is given by,

$$m_{j1} = \sum_{d_i \in g_j}\left(d_i - \lfloor <g_j> \rfloor\right) \text{ and } m_{j2} = \sum_{d_i \in g_j}\left(d_i - \lceil <g_j> \rceil\right)$$

where $<g_j>$ is the average value of all the degrees in that group. It can be easily inferred that if $M_{p \times 2}$ is a zero matrix, then the network is already *k*-anonymous. Finally, a *p*-dimensional solution vector should be computed where each element $m_j$ is chosen either from $m_{j1}$ or $m_{j2}$. The cost function is $\left|\sum_{j=1}^{p} m_j\right|$ and the closer it is to zero, better is the solution. This process has a computation cost of $O(2^q)$ where $q$ is the number of groups with $m_j \neq 0$. In [1], Casas-Roma et al. have proposed exhaustive and greedy methods to solve this problem.

- **Exhaustive Method:** By using exhaustive search, we select either $m_{j1}$ or $m_{j2}$ for $j = \{1, ..., p\}$ so that the minimum value of cost function is obtained. We consider all possible combinations unless a solution is found with zero cost function value.
- **Greedy Method:** In this method, values for $m_j$ are selected according to a probability distribution based on the size of $m_{j1}$ and $m_{j2}$. The probability of selection is given by the formula,

$$p(m_j = m_{j1}) = 1 - \left( \frac{m_{j1}}{m_{j1} + m_{j2}} \right)$$

$$p(m_j = m_{j2}) = 1 - \left( \frac{m_{j2}}{m_{j1} + m_{j2}} \right)$$

There lower the value of $m_{j1}$ or $m_{j2}$, higher is the probability of it being chosen. The process ends when the cost function reaches zero or when there is no improvement in the cost function.

## Graph Modification

We must modify the edges of the network so that it satisfies the anonymous $k$- anonymous degree sequence $\tilde{d}$. Three basic edge modifications are performed in this algorithm:

- **Edge Switch:** Edge switch among three vertices $v_i, v_j, v_k \in V$ where there existed an edge between $v_i$ and $v_j$ but not between $v_j$ and $v_k$ is defined by removing the $(v_i, v_j)$ edge and adding $(v_j, v_k)$ edge. After the process, $\tilde{d}_i = d_i - 1$ and $\tilde{d}_j = d_j + 1$. This operation preserves the number of edges in the network. See Figure 1(a).

*Figure 1. Edge switch (a), edge removal (b), and edge addition (c). Dotted lines indicated the deleted edges and solid lines indicate the added edges.*

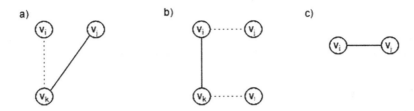

- **Edge Removal:** Edge removal between four vertices $v_i, v_j, v_k, v_l \in V$ where only edges $(v_i, v_j)$ and $(v_k, v_l)$ originally exist. We delete these edges and add $(v_i, v_k)$. After the process, $\tilde{d}_i = d_i$, $\tilde{d}_j = d_j - 1$, $\tilde{d}_k = d_k$ and $\tilde{d}_l = d_l - 1$. This operation reduces the number of edges in the network by 1. See Figure 1(b).
- **Edge Addition:** Edge addition between two vertices $(v_i, v_j) \in V$ having no edge between them involves adding an edge between them. After the process, $\tilde{d}_i = d_i + 1$ and $\tilde{d}_j = d_j + 1$. This operation increases the number of edges in the network by 1. See Figure 1(c).

The graph modification algorithm starts by computing $\delta = \tilde{d} - d$, which indicates how much each vertex's degree must be changed to achieve $k$-anonymity. $\delta$ is split into $\delta^-$ which includes the list of vertices which must decrease their degree and $\delta^+$ which includes the list of vertices which must increase their degree. We also compute $\sigma(d) = \sum_{i=1}^{n} d_i$ and $\sigma(\tilde{d}) = \sum_{i=1}^{n} \tilde{d}_i$. Based on $\sigma(d)$ and $\sigma(\tilde{d})$ we have four different graph modification scenarios:

1. If $\sigma(d) = \sigma(\tilde{d})$, then both the original network and the anonymized network have the same number of edges so we cannot apply *Edge Removal* or *Edge Addition* but only *Edge Switch* if necessary.
2. If $\sigma(\tilde{d}) < \sigma(d)$, then the anonymized network has lesser edges than the original network. The number of edges to be deleted is $\left| \dfrac{\sigma(d) - \sigma(\tilde{d})}{2} \right|$.

   *Edge Removal* is applied by finding two vertices $v_i, v_j \in \delta^-$ and two other vertices $v_k, v_l$ such that $(v_i, v_k) \in E$ and $(v_j, v_l) \in E$. These two edges are deleted and a new edge $(v_k, v_l)$ is added.

3. If $\sigma(\tilde{d}) > \sigma(d)$, we need to increase $\left| \dfrac{\sigma(d) - \sigma(\tilde{d})}{2} \right|$ number of edges to the network. We apply *Edge Addition* by selecting a pair of vertices $v_i, v_j$ such that $(v_i, v_j) \notin E$ and add an edge between them.

4. Until $\sigma(\tilde{d}) = \sigma(d) = 0$, we have to modify the degree of vertices through *Edge Switch* process. For each $v_i \in \delta^-$ and $v_j \in \delta^+$, we find another vertex $v_k$ such that $(v_i, v_k) \in E$. We delete this edge and create a new one $(v_k, v_j)$. The auxiliary edges require for graph modification can be selected by two approaches:

   a. **Random Edge Selection:** In this approach, random auxiliary edges $(v_i, v_k)$ and $(v_j, v_l)$ for edge deletion and $(v_i, v_k)$ for edge switch. This is the fastest approach but some important edges can be removed or new bridge-like edges can be created affecting considerably the local or global structure of the resulting network.

   b. **Neighborhood Edge Centrality Selection:** In this approach, the importance of each edge is taken into consideration. By removing or creating low relevance edges, we can achieve low information loss. The neighborhood centrality of an edge $(v_i, v_j)$ given by $NC_{\{v_i, v_j\}}$ is defined as the fraction of vertices which are neighbors of $v_i$ or $v_j$ but not of $v_i$ and $v_j$ simultaneously. Its formula is given by,

$$NC_{\{v_i, v_j\}} = \frac{\left| \Gamma(v_i) \cup \Gamma(v_j) \right| - \left| \Gamma(v_i) \cap \Gamma(v_j) \right|}{2 \max(degree)}$$

Consider a raw social network graph in Figure 2(a). It's degree sequence $d = \{2,4,2,1,3,2,2,2,2\}$ and when ordered it becomes $d = \{1,2,2,2,2,2,2,3,4\}$. We will analyze the anonymization process using UMGA Algorithm for $k = 2$. The optimal partition $g$ is obtained as $\{(1,2,2), (2,2), (2,2), (3,4)\}$. Since we get 4 groups, $p$ is 4. The matrix of differences is,

*Figure 2. Raw social network (a), 2-anonymous network using random edge selection (b) and 2-anonymous network using neighborhood edge centrality selection*

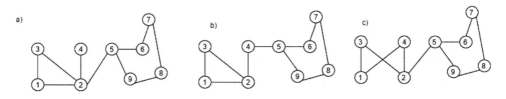

$$M_{p \times 2} = M_{4 \times 2} = \begin{pmatrix} 2 & -1 \\ 0 & 0 \\ 0 & 0 \\ 1 & -1 \end{pmatrix}$$

The first group (1,2,2) generates the first row (2, -1) in the matrix. The average degree of the group $< g_1 >$ is 1.67 which is floored to 1 for the first column and ceiled to 2 in the second column. Using the formulas for $m_{j1}$ and $m_{j2}$, we get $m_{11} = 0+1+1 = 2$ and $m_{12} = -1+0+0 = -1$. The other three rows of the matrix are computed using the same procedure. Next, we need to compute the anonymous degree sequence $\tilde{d}$. The exhaustive method explores all the set of possible $p$-vectors which are $\{2,0,0,1\}$, $\{2,0,0, -1\}$, $\{-1,0,0,1\}$ and $\{-1,0,0, -1\}$. The sum of degree values in first and second solutions are not even so they produce invalid solutions. The third and fourth solutions give vectors $\{2,2,2,2,2,2,2,2,3,3\}$ and $\{2,2,2,2,2,2,2,4,4\}$ which are both 2-anonymous sequences. We choose the former solution because it gives $\Delta$ as zero and preserves the number of edges in the original graph. The greedy method selects the solution according to the probability distribution from the matrix $M_{4 \times 2}$ which is

$$P\left(M_{4 \times 2}\right) = \begin{pmatrix} 0.33 & 0.67 \\ - & - \\ - & - \\ 0.5 & 0.5 \end{pmatrix}$$

The second and third rows do not have any value because they are zero rows in the matrix $M_{4\times2}$, so we don't need any modification. Using the two-degree unordered anonymous sequence {2,3,2,2,3,2,2,2,2} from which we get $\delta$ as {0, -1,0,1,0,0,0,0,0}. Therefore $\delta^-$ is vertex 2 and $\delta^+$ is vertex 4. $\sigma(d) = \sigma(\tilde{d})$ so only *Edge Switch* is necessary. Under random edge selection, we can randomly select vertex 5 to be the auxiliary vertex. $(v_2, v_5)$ is removed and $(v_4, v_5)$ is added as shown in Figure 2(b). When we used neighborhood edge centrality selection, we get the centrality scores of the possible candidates $(v_2, v_5)$, $(v_1, v_2)$ and $(v_2, v_3)$ as 0.875, 0.5 and 0.5 respectively. We can choose either one of the lowest scores. Figure 2(c) shows the resulting network when $(v_1, v_2)$ is removed and $(v_1, v_4)$ is added.

As for complexity, computing the optimal partition $g$ takes $O(\max(n \log n, k^2 n))$ (Hansen & Mukherjee, 2003) computing the $p$-vector from the matrix of differences $M_{p\times2}$ is NP for the exhaustive method and $O(wq)$ for the greedy method where $w$ is the number of fixed iterations and $q$ is the number of groups with $m_j \neq 0$. Graph modification is a P-problem for random edge selection and NP for neighborhood centrality edge selection, but it can be resolved in polynomial time by computing $\log_2$ of all possible combinations.

# CONSTRAINED PERTURBATION

Under this category, graph modification approaches use edge addition and deletion to meet some desired constraints. Many algorithms have been surveyed in Casas, Herrera-Joancomartí, and Torra (2017). We will look at one algorithm in particular called the Fast K-degree Anonymization algorithm which is quite efficient for large networks.

## Fast K-Degree Anonymization (FKDA) Algorithm

Lu et al. (2012) had proposed an algorithm called the FKDA algorithm which anonymizes a given social network through edge additions alone. The basic principle of the algorithm is to cluster the vertices into groups where each group contains at least $k$ vertices. The graph is then modified to ensure that the vertices in each group have the same degree. Low degree anonymization cost occurs when vertices with similar degrees are grouped together and for this purpose we arrange the vertices according to descending order of their degrees before applying the algorithm. The FKDA algorithm builds on three separate algorithms *greedy_examination, edge_creation* and *relaxed_edge creation*. We shall look deeply into these algorithms first.

## greedy_examination Algorithm

This algorithm clusters vertices into different anonymization groups. An anonymization group is the smallest subset of order vertices set $v$ that has at least k members and its member degrees are higher than those of the remaining vertices. The cost of subsequent anonymization of the group is the sum of residual degrees after anonymization. For example, an anonymized group $(v_i, ..., v_j)$ in descending order of their degrees is given by the formula $\sum_{l=i}^{j}(d_i - d_l)$ where $d_l$ is the degree of vertex $v_l$. It takes input a sequence of vertices $v$ of length $n$ sorted in descending order, an index $i$ such that the vertex sequence $(v_1, v_2, ..., v_{i-1})$ has been $k$-anonymous and the value of $k$. It outputs an integer $n_a$ such that vertices $(v_i, v_{i+1}, ..., v_{i+n_a-1})$ are selected to be clustered into an anonymized group. The value of $n_a$ depends on the vertex sequence $v$. For in-depth explanation regarding the values assigned to $n_a$ for the various cases can be referred in Liu et al. (2012). The pseudocode is given below:

*Algorithm greedy_examination*

**Input:** sorted vertex sequence $v$, index $i$ and the value of $k$ for $k$-anonymity.

**Output:** $n_a$ which is the number of consecutive vertices that are going to be anonymized.

1. Find the first vertex $v_j$ such that $d_j < d_i$
2. **if** $v_j$ is not found **then**
3. $n_a = n - i + 1$
4. **else**
5. **if** $d_j = d_i - 1$ **then**
6. **if** $n - j + 1 < k$ **then** $n_a = n - i + 1$
7. **else** $n_a = j - i$
8. **end** if-else

9.  **else**
10. **if** $n - i + 1 < 2k$ **or** $n - j + 1 < k$ **then** $n_a = n - i + 1$
11. **else** $n_a =$ max $(k, j - i)$
12. **end** if-else
13. **end** if-else
14. **end** if-else
15. Return $n_a$

## edge_creation Algorithm

The main purpose of this algorithm is to anonymize vertices $v_i, v_{i+1}, ..., v_{i+n_a-1}$ to degree $d_i$ by adding edges. It outputs an index, which is $i + n_a$ if the anonymization succeeds, or equals j if $v_j$ cannot be anonymized, where $i <$ $j \le i + n_a - 1$. This algorithm wires each $v_j$ in the sequence $v_i, v_{i+1}, ..., v_{i+n_a-1}$ to $v_l$ for $j < l \le n$ such that edge $(j, l)$ did not originally exist (avoids creating multiple edges)and $d_l < d_i$ until $d_j = d_i$ (minimizes the need for reordering $v$ ). Three heuristics are considered to examine the candidate vertices in $v$ for the creation of edges. The first heuristics examines $v$ from $v_{j+1}$ to $v_n$ and creates the edge $(j, l)$ whenever the constraint is satisfied (has the largest anonymization cost). The second heuristics examines $v$ from $v_n$ to $v_{j+1}$ (has the least anonymization cost). The last heuristics randomly selects a candidature $v_l$ and creates the edge $(j, l)$. The pseudocode for this algorithm is given below:

### Algorithm edge_creation

**Input:** sorted vertex sequence $v$ and $n_a$ which is the number of vertices that are going to be anonymized starting from $v_i$ .

    **Output:** j, an index.

1.  **for** $j \in (i + 1, i + n_a - 1)$ **do**
2.  **while** $d_j < d_i$ **do**
3.  Create an edge $(j, l)$ where $j < l \le n$ such that $(j, l)$ does not previously exist and $d_l < d_i$
4.  **if** the edge cannot be created **then** return j
5.  **end** if

6.    **end** while
7.    **end** for
8.    Sort $v$ in the descending order of degrees
9.    return j

If *edge_creation* can anonymize these $n_a$ vertices, it reorders the new vertex sequence $v$ in the descending order of their degrees. If not, it returns the index j such that $v_j$ cannot be anonymized with the wiring constraint in which case, the repairing algorithm *relaxed_edge creation* is invoked.

## relaxed_edge creation Algorithm

The main purpose of this algorithm is to relax the wiring constant which prevents *edge_creation* from creating a *k*-anonymous graph. $v$ is examined from $v_n$ to $v_1$, iteratively adding edge (j, $l$) if the edge did not originally exist until $d_j = d_i$. Once this process is finished, the index $l$ is returned is fed to *greedy_examination* for the next iteration after sorting. If the returned $l$ is less than i, then *k*-degree anonymity of the sequence $v_1, v_2, ..., v_{i-1}$ would be compromised because $v_j$ would be wired to some vertex which was already anonymized. In this case, i is set as 0 so that *greedy_examination* examines $v$ from the beginning. When the returned $l$ is greater than i, *greedy_examination* examines $v$ from $v_i$. The pseudocode for this algorithm is given below:

*Algorithm relaxed_edge creation*
**Input:** sorted vertex sequence $v$ and indices i, j
    **Output:** an index $l$

1.    **for** $l = $ n to 1 **do**
2.    **if** $v_j$ and $v_l$ are not connected **then**
3.    Create an edge (j, $l$)
4.    **if** $d_j = d_i$ **then**
5.    Sort $v$ in the descending order of degrees
6.    return $l$
7.    **end** if
8.    **end** if
9.    **end** for

## FKDA Algorithm

We are now ready to look at the Fast K-degree Anonymous (FKDA) algorithm that combines all the three algorithms mentioned above. At every iteration, FKDA invokes the *greedy_examination* algorithm to compute the value of $n_a$ and passes it to *edge_creation* algorithm along with the value of index $i$. If *edge_creation* is able to successfully anonymize $n_a$ vertices then FKDA outputs the anonymized graph G' if $i >$ n, if not it enters into the next iteration. If *edge_creation* fails, FKDA invokes *relaxed_edge creation* and updates $i$ according to the value of $l$ returned by *relaxed_edge creation*. Note that FKDA can always output a valid $k$-anonymous graph because even in the worst case a complete graph is created. The pseudocode for FKDA is given below:

### Algorithm FKDA

**Input:** input graph G with n vertices and the value of $k$ for $k$-anonymity
  **Output:** G' which is a $k$-anonymous version of G

1.   $v =$ the vertex sequence of G in the descending order of degrees
2.   i = 1
3.   **while** i ≤ n **do**
4.   $n_a = greedy\_examination$ ($v$, i, $k$)
5.   j = *edge_creation* ($v$, i, $n_a$)
6.   **if** j = i + $n_a$ **then**
7.   i = i + $n_a$
8.   **else**
9.   $l = relaxed\_edge\ creation$ ($v$, i, j)
10.   **if** $l <$ i **then** i = 0
11.   **end** if-else
12.   **end** while
13.   return G'

Experimental results conducted in Liu et al. (2012) indicate that FKDA is more efficient and effective on larger networks than KDA algorithm proposed by Liu et al. (2008). A significant factor causing poor efficiency in KDA algorithm is the need for realizability testing which is eliminated in FKDA.

# ACHIEVING ANONYMITY THROUGH NOISE NODES

## k - Degree and *l*-Diversity

Yuan et al. (2013) introduced an anonymization model which adds additional low degree nodes called noise nodes to achieve $k$-anonymity and $l$-diversity. Most social networks satisfy the power law distribution (Barbasi & Albert, 1999), therefore there exists many low degree vertices in the graph which could be used to hide added noise nodes from being identified. Inserting noise nodes can protect some graph properties than pure-edge editing method. We will first look at the $k$-degree $l$- diversity (KDLD) model which was proposed along with the noise node algorithms in Yuan et al. (2013). Given an input graph G, its sensitive degree sequence P is a sequence of n triples P[1], …, P[n] where each P[i] is a triple(id, d, s) at position i in P where 'd' and 's' are the degree and sensitive label of the node 'id'. $p_j$ represents node j's triple in P and $p_j.d$ refers to its degree. KDLD sequence is a sequence which satisfies both $k$-anonymity and $l$ -diversity. We need to obtain an optimum KDLD sequence $P^{new}$ of the input graph which is the one with the minimum Loss function $L(P, P^{new}) = \sum_{\forall u} | p_u.d - p_u^{new}.d |$ which ensures that small degree change is required so that fewer noise nodes are required.

## KDLD Sequence Generation

In order to create the KDLD sequence, two algorithms were proposed: K-L based and L-K based. Initially, the triples in P are divided into groups and all the corresponding vertices of the same group shall be adjusted to have the same degree which is called the target degree. The target degree of a group is considered as the mean degree of the group.

- Algorithm K-L based selects the first $k$ elements in P as a group and adds vertices until $l$- diversity is satisfied.
- Algorithm L-K based satisfies $l$- diversity first by grouping $l$ vertices with different labels and similar degrees. Then vertices with similar degrees are added to the group until the group has $k$ elements to satisfy $k$-anonymity as well.

After a group satisfies k-anonymity and $l$- diversity two costs are calculated:

- $C_{new}$: It is the cost for creating a new group for the next $k$ elements which is the total degree change that makes all the vertices in the group have the same degree.
- $C_{merge}$: It is the cost of merging the next element into the current group and creating a new group for the next $k$ elements by skipping the next element.

If $C_{new}$ is smaller, then we create a new group and if $C_{merge}$ is smaller, then we merge the next element into the current group. At any time, if the remaining elements are less than $k$ or contain less than $l$ distinct sensitive labels, they are merged into the last group. The KDLD sensitive degree sequence $P^{new}$ is then fed to the graph construction algorithm.

## Graph Construction

We need to construct an anonymized graph G' such that the subset of P'(sensitive degree sequence of G') having only the vertices in G called $P_o'$ is equal to $P^{new}$. The anonymous graph is modified in 5 steps which each step serving a unique purpose.

## Step 1: Neighborhood Edge Editing Technique

In this step, we first try to change node's degrees by adding or deleting edges making sure that the distance between the two nodes change by 1 only. This algorithm works in 3 cases:

**Case 1:** If a node u need to increase its degree and node v needs to decrease its degree to attain target degree and (u, v) are direct neighbors then we randomly select a direct neighbor w of v that is not connected to u and add an edge between u and w and remove an edge between w and v.

**Case 2:** If there are two nodes u, v which are two hop neighbors and both need to increase their degree to attain the target degree then we add an edge between u and v if there was no edge initially

**Case 3:** If there are two nodes u, v which need to decrease their degree to attain the target degree and removing an edge still makes these two nodes two hop neighbors, then remove the edge.

The pseudocode for this algorithm is given below:

1.  **for** each node $u$ that needs to increase degree **do**
2.      $d = u$'s degree
3.      $d' = u$'s target degree
4.      **for** $i$ from 0 to $d' - d$ **do**
5.      Find $v, w$ that has links $(u, v)$ and $(v, w)$ where $v$ needs to decrease degree
6.      **if** such $v, w$ exists **then**
7.      Remove $(v, w)$
8.      Add link $(u, w)$
9.      **else**
10.     break
11.     **end** if-else
12.     **end** for
13.     **end** for
14.     **for** each node $u$ that needs to increase degree **do**
15.     **for** each node $v$ that needs to increase degree **do**
16.     **if** $u, v$ are 2 hop neighbors **then**
17.     **if** $u, v$ do not have a link **then**
18.     Add link $(u, v)$
19.     **end** if
20.     **end** if
21.     **end** for
22.     **end** for
23.     **for** each node $u$ that needs to increase degree **do**
24.     **for** each node $v$ that needs to increase degree **do**
25.     **if** $u, v$ do have a link **then**
26.     Remove link $(u, v)$
27.     **end** if
27.     **if** $u, v$ are no longer 2 hop neighbors **then**
28.     Add back link $(u, v)$
29.     **end** if
30.     **end** for
31.     **end** for

## Step 2: Adding Noise Node to Decrease Degree

In case there is any node $u$ whose degree is still larger than its target degree, we need to perform this step.

- Create a new node (noise node) $n$ and connect it to $u$ which makes $n.d = 1$ and $u.d = p_u.d + 1$. Create a new variable $temp$ which is equal to $u.d + 2 - p'_u.d$. This value is assigned to $temp$ because $u's$ degree is changed through $n$ so $n$ has a degree of $temp$ once the process is completed.

- Now we need to set $n's$ target degree $target_{new}$ to a degree in $P'$. If $temp$ is less than the minimum degree in $P'$, set $target_{new}$ as this degree. Otherwise, set the closest degree in $P'$ which is lesser than $temp$ as the $target_{new}$.

- Next, randomly select an edge $(u, v)$ present in the original network. Delete this edge and connect it through $n$ by adding edge $(n, v)$. This chances the distance between $u$ and $v$ from 1 to 2. Repeat this procedure until $u.d = p'_u.d$. Note that when $n.d = target_{new}$, we create a new noise node and follow the same procedure.

Consider an example given in Figure 3(a). Suppose we need to decrease node $u's$ degree from 3 to 2. Two nodes $v_1$ and $v_2$ are chosen. We disconnect these nodes from $u$ and connect them to $n$. This reduces $u's$ degree by 1. The pseudo code for this algorithm is given below:

1. **for** every node $u$ that needs to decrease degree **do**
2. $d = u's$ degree
3. $target =$ target degree of $u$
4. **while** *true* **do**
5. Select a sensitive value $s$ from $u's$ one hop neighbor
6. Create a new node $n$ with sensitive value $s$
7. $d' = 1$
8. $target_{new} = Select\_closest\_deg\_in\_grp\,(d + 2 - the$ target degree$)$
9. Connect $u$ with $n$
10. $d = d + 1$
11. **while** *true* **do**
12. Randomly select a link $(u, v)$ from $G$
13. Delete $(u, v)$ and create $(n, v)$
14. $d' = d' + 1$
15. $d = d - 1$
16. **if** $d' ==$ target$_{new}$ **or** $d ==$ target **then**
17. *break*

18.  **end** if
19.  **end** while
20.  **if** $d ==$ target **then**
21.  *break*
22.  **end** if
23.  **end** while
24.  **end** for

## Step 3: Adding Noise Node to Increase Degree

For every node $u$ which needs to increase its degree, we need to perform this step. We first find another node $v$ which also needs to increase its degree within two hop distance from $u$. The noise nodes added in step 2 are also included in the search procedure. We join $u$ and $v$ to a new noise node $n$. After this procedure, if $n's$ degree is greater than the minimum degree in $P^{new}$ and does not appear in $P^{new}$, we recursively delete the last link until it reaches a degree in $P^{new}$. Otherwise, we leave $n$ to process in Step 4. The pseudo code for this algorithm is given below:

1.   **for** every node $u$ that needs to increase degree **do**
2.   **for** i =0; i< *increase_num*; i++ do
3.   Create a new node $n$
4.   Connect node $u$ with $n$
5.   **for** every node $v$ within two hop distance from $u$ **do**
6.   **if** $v$ needs to increase its degree **then**
7.   connect $v$ to $n$
8.   **end** if
9.   **end** for
10.  **while** $n's$ degree not in $P'$ or $n's$ degree is greater than min degree in group **do**
11.  remove the last connection created to $n$
12.  i = i -1
13.  **end** while
14.  **end** for
15.  **end** for

## Step 4: Adjusting Noise Node Degree

In this step, we adjust the noise node degrees so that it matches with those in $P^{new}$. This ensures original and noise nodes are indistinguishable. We first find pair of noise nodes which need to increase degree within three hop distance from each other and connect them. Noise nodes within three hops are either connected to the same node or are connected to two directly connected nodes in the original graph. After this process, we select the noise nodes which need to still increase degree and if it has an even degree, we select the closest bigger even degree in $P^{new}$ as its target degree. For odd degree noise nodes, we choose the closest bigger odd degree. We then select randomly a nearest edge to the noise node, remove it from the graph and connect the endpoints of this edge to the noise node which increases its degree by 2. "nearest" edge to a noise node $n$ is an edge whose average distance of the two points in the edge $(u, v)$ is minimum among all edges. Since both the end points of the removed edge are near the noise node, connecting them directly to the noise node not only makes them stay in the neighborhood of the noise node but changes the length of paths through these endpoints only by 1. This process is repeated until the noise node's degree reaches the target degree. Figure 3 (b) describes this procedure. The pseudo code for this algorithm is given below:

1.   Select pair of noise nodes that are within three hops of each other and build a link between them
2.   **for** every noise node $n$ with even degree **do**
3.   Select the closest bigger even degree in $P^{new}$ as $\text{target}_{new}$

*Figure 3. (a) Step 2 (decrease degree), (b) Step 4 (Adjust degree). Solid line is an edge originally present, dashed line is an edge originally present but removed and dotted line indicates an added edge.*

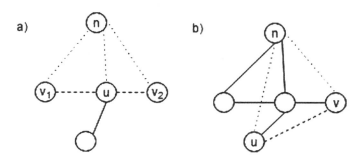

4.   **end** for
5.   **for** every noise node $n$ with odd degree **do**
6.   Select the closest bigger odd degree in $P^{new}$ as target$_{new}$
7.   **end** for
8.   **for** each noise node $n$ **do**
9.   **while** $n.d \neq$ target$_{new}$ **do**
10.  Find a nearest edge $(u, v)$ to $n$
11.  Remove $(u, v)$
12.  Connect $u$ and $v$ to $n$
13.  **end** while
14.  **end** for

## Step 5: Noise Node Label

Since each degree group already satisfies $l$- diversity, the noise node can take any sensitive label. Typically, we randomly find a neighbor node $v$ of $u$ which is the original node for which the noise node was created and assign $v's$ sensitive label to it.

Yuan *et al. (2013)* have extended their approach to include recursive (c, l) diversity as well. To minimize the loss function L(P, P$^{new}$), we need to ensure that a same degree group $C$ satisfies safety grouping condition which requires three conditions to be satisfied:

1.   $C \geq k$;
2.   $f_1 < c(f_\ell + f_{\ell+1} + ... + f_m)$;
3.   $\dfrac{f_1 + 1}{f_1(m - \ell + 1)} < c$.

When pure edge-editing method is used, safety grouping condition contains only the first two constraints. Given the degree sequence $P$, at every iteration, we create a new group $C$ for $P[0]$, remove $P[0]$ out of $P$ and store its degree in a variable $d$. Then we recursively check the next element and add it to $C$ only if its degree is also $d$ or if its label does not appear in top $L - 1$ times in $C$. Once an element is added, it is removed from $P$ and we start checking again from the head of $P$ since the label occurrence numbers could have changed. This process is continued till $C$ satisfies the safety grouping condition. When this condition is satisfied, $C$ is added to $P^{new}$ and a new group is created. If there exists any group that cannot satisfy this condition, we store it in a set R and for each node in $R$ we add it to an existing group if that group satisfies safety grouping condition after the node is added. The pseudocode for this algorithm is given below:

**Input:** $P$ which is the sensitive degree sequence of the graph

**Output:** $P^{new}$ which is the new sensitive degree sequence that satisfies recursive $(c, l)$ diversity

1.    $P$ = Sensitive degree sequence of the original graph G
2.    Set $R = \{\}$
3.    **while** $|P| > 0$ **do**
4.    Group $C = \{P[0]\}$
5.    $d = P[0].d$
6.    Remove $P[0]$ from $P$
7.    **while** C does not satisfy Safety Grouping Condition **do**
8.    **for** i=0;i<$|P|$; i++ **do**
9.    **if** $P[i].d \equiv d$ **then**
10.   $C = C \cup \{P[i]\}$
11.   Remove $P[i]$ from $P$
12.   break
13.   **else**
14.   **if** $P[i].s$ is not in top $l - 1$ appearance label set of $C$ **then**
15.   $C = C \cup \{P[i]\}$
16.   Remove $P[i]$ from $P$
17.   break
18.   **end** if
19.   **end** if-else
20.   **end** for
21.   **if** i == $|P|$ **then**
22.   $R = R \cup C$
23.   break
24.   **end** if
25.   **end** while
26.   Set the target degrees of elements in $C$ as corresponding node's mean degree
27.   Copy $C$ into $P^{new}$ if C satisfies Safety Grouping Condition
28.   **end** while
29.   Assign the elements in R into existing groups

Once the recursive (c, $l$) diversity sequence is generated, we need a new algorithm to assign sensitive labels to the noise nodes created. Two basic steps are followed:

- First assign labels to the noise nodes by following the label distribution of the original nodes in the group.
- Then if the recursive (c, $l$) diversity is not satisfied, assign the least frequent label in the group to the noise node which was assigned the most frequent label. By doing this, we reduce the most frequent label's occurrence by 1 and increase the least frequent label's occurrence by 1. This procedure is repeated until the group satisfies recursive (c, $l$) diversity.

The pseudocode for this algorithm is given below:

1.  **for** each same degree group C **do**
2.  Group $C_0$ = group of original nodes in $C$
3.  Group $C_n$ = group of noise nodes in $C$
4.  Array $L_0$ = sensitive labels on the nodes in $C_0$
5.  Array $N_0$ = $L_0$'s occurrence numbers in $C_0$
6.  Array $N_n$ = an array with size $|L_0|$
7.  **for** i =0; i < $|L_0|$; i++ **do**
8.  $N_n[i] = \left\lceil |C_n| \times \dfrac{N_0[i]}{|C_0|} \right\rceil$
9.  **end** for
10. **if** $\sum_{i=0}^{|N_n|-1} N_n[i] < |C_n|$ **then**
11. Compute $\max$ where $N_0[\max]$ is the maximum value in $N_0$
12. $N_n[\max] = N_n[\max] + |C_n| - \sum_{i=0}^{|N_n|-1} N_n[i]$
13. **end** if
14. **while** $\neg(\,N_0 + N_n$ satisfies recursive (c, $l$) diversity) **do**
15. Compute $\min$ where $N_n[\min] + N_0[\min]$ is the minimum value in $N_0 + N_n$
16. Compute $\max$ where $N_n[\max] + N_0[\max]$ is the minimum value in $N_0 + N_n$
17. $N_n[\max] = N_n[\max] - 1$
18. $N_n[\min] = N_n[\min] - 1$

19. **end** while
20. Assign labels to noise nodes in $C_n$ where $\forall i$, $N_n[i]$ noise nodes have label $L_0[i]$
21. **end** for

## α-ANONYMIZATION

Motivated by the noise node algorithms we proposed a technique in Chakraborty and Tripathy (2016) to achieve α-anonymization in social networks by adding noise nodes. Eigen vector centrality concept is used to preserve the social importance of nodes. We arrange the nodes in an eigenvector centrality based sequence (EVCS) which is a non-decreasing order representation of the nodes based on their eigenvector centrality value. Suppose a graph G has $m$ nodes then its EVCS is an order n[1].evc≥n[2].evc≥...n[$m$].evc where n[i].evc is the eigenvector centrality value of the i$^{\text{th}}$ node.

## (α, k) ANONYMITY

Our algorithm initially creates a temporary group $G_{temp}$ and adds elements to it from the EVCS until the group satisfies (α, k) anonymity. (α, k) anonymity is satisfied by first achieving k-anonymity and then satisfying the α-deassociation property. In case we run out of elements to add, we merge the group with a previously created group such that the group still satisfies (α, k) anonymity after merging. In the pseudocode of the algorithm given below, $G_{ki}$ denotes the i-th group that satisfies k-anonymity.

**Input:** EVCS
**Output:** (α, k) anonymous sequence

1. Set i=0, $G_{temp}$ = { }
2. **while** |EVCS| > 0 **do**
3. **while** (|Gtemp | < k && |EVCS| > 0) **do**
4. $G_{temp} = G_{temp} \cup$ EVCS [0]
5. Remove EVCS [0] from EVCS

6.   **end** while
7.   **if** (|Gtemp | ≥ k) **then**
8.   Set *alphaDeassociated* =true
9.   **while** ($G_{temp}$ does not satisfy alpha-deassociation) **do**
10.  **if** (|EVCS|>0) **then**
11.  $G_{temp} = G_{temp} \cup EVCS[0]$
12.  Remove EVCS[0] from EVCS
13.  **alphaDeassociated = True**
14.  **end** if
15.  **else**
16.  *alphaDeassociated* = False
17.  break
18.  **end** while
19.  **if** (*alphaDeassociated*) **then**
20.  Set $G_{ki} = G_{temp}$ && increment i by 1
21.  Delete the elements in $G_{temp}$
22.  **end** if
23.  **else**
24.  Set size= i
25.  Add $G_{temp}$ to the $G_{ksize}$
26.  **while** ($G_{ksize}$ does not satisfy alpha deassociation) **do**
27.  Set newsize = size-1
28.  Add $G_{ksize}$ to $G_{knewsize}$ && reduce size by 1
29.  **end** while
30.  **end** else
31.  **end** if
32.  **else**
33.  size= i
34.  Add $G_{temp}$ to the $G_{ksize}$
35.  while ($G_{ksize}$ does not satisfy alpha deassociation) do
36.  Set newsize = size-1
37.  Add $G_{ksize}$ to $G_{knewsize}$ && reduce size by 1
38.  **end** while
39.  **end** else
40.  **end** while

## (α, *l*) DIVERSITY

The algorithm is very similar to the (α, k) anonymity algorithm with just two steps changed. In step 3 we check for *l*- diversity along with k-anonymity so the step becomes:

**while** ((|$G_{temp}$| < k or $G_{temp}$ does not satisfy *l*- diversity) && |EVCS|>0) **do**

In step 7 we verify *l*- diversity condition before checking if the group satisfies α-deassociation, so the step becomes:

**if** (|$G_{temp}$| ≥ k and $G_{temp}$ satisfies *l*- diversity) **then**

By changing these two steps, the algorithm can anonymize a social network to satisfy (α, *l*) diversity. We ran our algorithms on a synthetically created dataset and a real dataset. The Synthetic Erdos-Renyi Graph (ER Graph) has 1000 vertices and 5000 edges. The real dataset is a co-authorship dataset compiled by Newman (2006). It has 1589 vertices and 2742 edges. α has been kept at a constant value of 0.5 in all our experiments. It can be seen from Figure 4 that our approach achieved least change in APL from the raw graph compared to other methods. Figure 5 shows our (α, *l*) diversity algorithm results on the real dataset.

*Figure 4. (α, k) anonymity on ER graph*

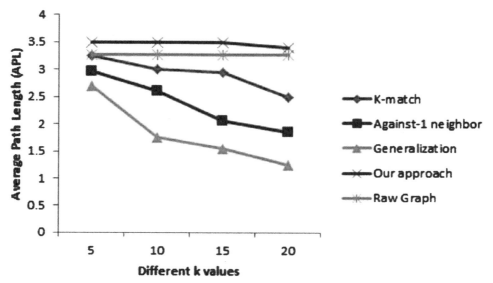

*Figure 5. (α, l) diversity on the real dataset*

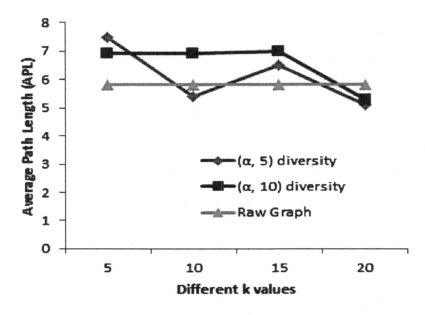

*Figure 6. Noise node EVC when k=5; EVC when k=10*

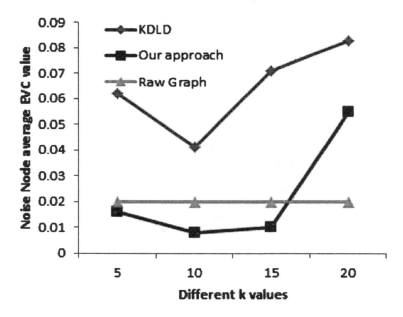

# RECURSIVE (α, c, *l*) DIVERSITY

An equivalence group satisfies recursive (α, c, *l*) diversity if it satisfies both alpha-deassociation property and recursive (c, *l*) diversity. The algorithm works in a similar manner like the (α, k) anonymity algorithm and we add an element to $G_{temp}$ only if its degree is similar or its sensitive label is not in the top *l* -1 appearance label set of $G$. In the algorithm $G_{temp}$ denotes a temporary group and $G_{rdi}$ is the i-th equivalence group that satisfies (α, c, *l*) diversity. The pseudocode for the algorithm is given below:

**Input:** EVCS

**Output:** recursive (α, c, *l*) diverse sequence

1.   Set R = { }
2.   **while** |EVCS | > 0 **do**
3.   $G_{temp}$ = EVCS[0]
4.   d=EVCS[0].d
5.   Remove EVCS [0] out of EVCS
6.   **while** ( $G_{temp}$ satisfies safety grouping condition) **do**
7.   **for** i=0; i < |EVCS|; i++ **do**
8.   **if** EVCS[i].d ≡ d **then**
9.   $G_{temp}$ = $G_{temp}$ ∪ EVCS[i]
10.  Remove EVCS[i] out of EVCS
11.  **break**
12.  **else if** EVCS[i].s is not in the top *l* -1 appearance label set of $G$ **then**
13.  $G_{temp}$ = $G_{temp}$ ∪ EVCS[i]
14.  Remove EVCS[i] out of EVCS
15.  **break**
16.  **if** i == |EVCS| **then**
17.  R = R ∪ $G_{temp}$
18.  **break**
19.  Set alphaDeassociated = *true*
20.  **while** ( $G_{temp}$ does not satisfy alpha deassociation) **do**
21.  **if** (|EVCS|>0) **then**
22.  $G_{temp}$ = $G_{temp}$ ∪ EVCS[0]
23.  Remove EVCS[0]from EVCS
24.  alphaDeassociated = *true*

25. **end** if
26. **else**
27. alphaDeassociated = *false*
28. **break**
29. **end** while
30. **if** (alphaDeassociated) **then**
31. Set $G_{rcli} = G_{temp}$ && increment i by 1
32. Delete the elements in $G_{temp}$
33. **end** if
34. **else**
35. Set size= i
36. Add $G_{temp}$ to the $G_{rclsize}$
37. **while** ( $G_{rclsize}$ does not satisfy alpha deassociation) **do**
38. Set newsize= size-1
39. Add $G_{rclsize}$ to $G_{rcl\ newsize}$ && reduce size by 1
40. **end** while
41. **end** else
42. **end** if
43. **else**

*Figure 7. Noise Node EVC when k=10*

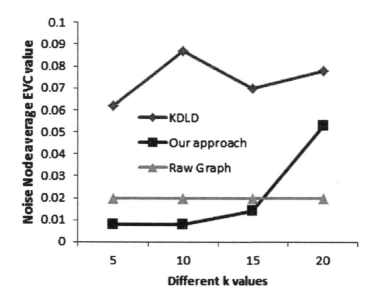

*Figure 8. APL for recursive (α, c, l) diversity*

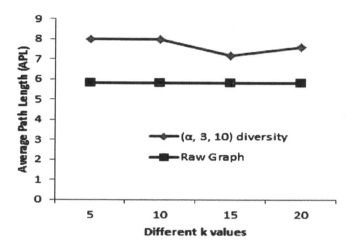

*Figure 9. Noise Node EVC when c =3 and l =10*

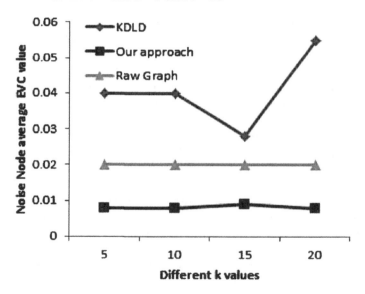

44.  size= i
45.  **Add** $G_{temp}$ to $G_{rclsize}$
46.  **while** ( $G_{rclsize}$ does not satisfy alpha deassociation) **do**
47.  Set newsize= size-1

48. Add $G_{rdsize}$ to $G_{rcl\ newsize}$ && reduce size by 1
49. **end** while
50. **end** else
51. **end** while

Figure 8 and Figure 9 contain the results of our recursive ($\alpha$, c, $l$) diversity algorithm on the real dataset. It can be inferred that our algorithm creates noise nodes which have less social importance better than the KDLD algorithm.

## REFERENCES

Barabasi, A. L., & Albert, R. (1999). Emergence of Scaling in Random Networks. *Science*, *286*(5439), 509–512. doi:10.1126/science.286.5439.509 PMID:10521342

Casas, R. J., Herrera-Joancomartí, J., & Torra, V. (2017). A survey of graph-modification techniques for privacy-preserving on networks. *Artificial Intelligence Review*, *47*(3), 341–366. doi:10.1007/s10462-016-9484-8

Casas-Roma, J., Herrera-Joancomartí, J., & Torra, V. (2016). k-Degree anonymity and edge selection: Improving data utility in large networks. *Knowledge and Information Systems*, 1–28. doi:10.1007/s10115-016-0947-7

Chakraborty, S., & Tripathy, B. K. (2016). Alpha-anonymization techniques for privacy preservation in social networks. *Social Network Analysis and Mining*, *6*(29), 1–11.

Hansen, S. L., & Mukherjee, S. (2003). A polynomial algorithm for optimal univariate micro-aggregation. *IEEE Transactions on Knowledge and Data Engineering*, *15*(4), 1043–1044. doi:10.1109/TKDE.2003.1209020

Liu, K., & Terzi, E. (2008). Towards identity anonymization on graphs. *SIGMOD Conference*, 93–106.

Lu, X., Song, Y., & Bressan, S. (2012). Fast identity anonymization on graphs. In *Proceedings of the 23rd international conference on database and expert systems applications*. Vienna, Austria: Springer.

Newman, M. E. (2006). Finding community structure in network using Eigen vectors. *Physical Review. E*, *74*(3), 036104. doi:10.1103/PhysRevE.74.036104 PMID:17025705

Yuan, M., Chen, L., Yu, P. S., & Yu, T. (2013, March). Protecting Sensitive Labels in Social Network Data Anonymization, Knowledge and Data Engineering. *IEEE Transactions on Knowledge and Data Engineering, 25*(3), 633–647. doi:10.1109/TKDE.2011.259

# Chapter 6
# Weighted and Directed Graph Approaches

## ABSTRACT

*It is interesting to look at the types of social networks that are directed or weighted, or social networks with the combination of both. In many cases, the relationship between vertices may be quantifiable (weighted) or asymmetrical (directed). In this chapter, the authors first introduce the concept of weighted social networks and present an anonymization algorithm for these networks called the anonymity generalization algorithm. After that, they discuss k-anonymous path privacy and introduce the MSP algorithm. Next, the authors introduce the (k1, k2)-shortest path privacy and a (k1, k2)-shortest path privacy algorithm. Then they introduce directed weighted social networks and present the k-multiple paths anonymization on PV+NV (KMPPN). Also, the authors present a technique to convert directed networks into undirected networks. Finally, the authors present the linear property preserving anonymization approach for social networks.*

## INTRODUCTION

So far, we have only seen undirected and unweighted social networks. While these networks contain the most amount of dedicated research, it is interesting to look at the other types of social networks like directed or weighted or social networks with the combination of both. In many cases, the relationship between vertices may be quantifiable (weighted) or asymmetrical (directed). Note that

DOI: 10.4018/978-1-5225-5158-4.ch006

most directed network algorithms can be applied to undirected networks by replacing the undirected edge with two directed edges but the vice-versa i.e. applying undirected network algorithms in directed networks is not applicable in many algorithms. It is essential to study these networks because certain important data structures in computer science such as trees, directed acyclic graphs and so on are not undirected. One important application of directed graphs is in cases where we do not wish to revisit the visited nodes again critical in fault diagnosis systems.

## WEIGHTED SOCIAL NETWORKS

Under this section, we will look at the various anonymization approaches proposed for undirected weighted social networks alone. The weight on edges can represent degree of friendship, trustworthiness, behaviour, etc. We will consider directed weighted social networks as a different section later. As stated in the introductory chapters, a weighted social network graph is one where the edges between vertices have quantifiable weights associated with them. It is given by $G = (V, E, W)$ where $V$ is the set of nodes, $E$ is the set of edges and $W$ is the matrix of weights associated with the edges such that $w_{a,b}$ is the weight in edge $e_{a,b}$ that connects nodes $a$ and $b$.

### Generalization Approach

We will begin with a simple generalization algorithm to achieve $k$-anonymity proposed by in Skarkala *et al.* (2012). Recall that generalization-based anonymization approaches cluster nodes into super-nodes and edges into super-edges. One of the major issues that arises while clustering weighted edges is to handle the weights between edges. Skarkala *et al. (2012)* have considered super-edge weights to be the average of the original edge weights in the super-edge. Given two super-nodes $sn_a$ and $sn_b$, super-edge probability $p_{sn_a, sn_b}$ is the probability of the existence of an edge between these nodes. The Information Loss considered between the original graph $G$ and the anonymized graph $G'$ is given by,

$$IL(G, G') = \sum_{(i,j) \in E} \left| W(i, j) - W'(i, j) \right|^2$$

where $W'(i,j)$ is the weight of the super-edge in $G'$ that represents edge $(i,j)$

The anonymization procedure works in 5 steps described below:

1. **Naïve Anonymization:** In this step, all the identifiers of the original graph $G$ are removed and replaced by temporary identities so that an adversary who does not possess any prior knowledge on $G$ cannot re-identify any targeted node, edge or edge weight.

2. **Node Anonymization:** This step involves grouping nodes into super-nodes based on their similarity and the strength of their relationship to other nodes. Super-nodes created must include at least k nodes to achieve k-anonymity.

3. **Edge Weight Computation:** Next we need to anonymize the edges in $G$. These edges are grouped and represented as super-edges in $G'$. The weights of these super-edges are the average weights of the original nodes with a possible addition of a random component for further anonymization of edge weights.

4. **Edge Anonymity:** Along with edge weights $w'$ computed in the previous step, the super-edges also have a probability of existence $p_{sn_a,sn_b}$ associated with them which defines the percentage of original edges that are represented by a super-edge. If this probability is greater than $p$ which is a user given parameter, then the probability is bounded by a threshold $p'$.

5. **Publication:** The final anonymized network $G'$ is then published to the outside world.

The pseudo-code of the algorithm is given below. The proposed algorithm initially considers each node $n_i$ in $G$ as a super-node $sn_i$ in $G'$ and the corresponding edges are created by steps 4 -6. When then select super-nodes $sn_i$ which have less then $k$ elements and use the *candidates* function to return a list of possible merger options. Nodes with shared neighbors are likely to have least loss induced, so the set of 2-hop neighbors of node $sn_i$ is used as candidates. If this set is empty, the set of neighbors constitutes the next attempted candidate set. If this set is empty, too, then all remaining super-nodes are used as candidates. Function *evaluate_merger* is used to calculate the information loss induced when we merge $sn_i$ with a possible candidate $sn_j$. Function *merge* creates a new super-node $sn_{new}$ by merging $sn_i$ with

$sn_j$, and it creates all super-edges related to this new super-node and assigns them the average weight $w'$ of the corresponding edges. The algorithm iterates until every super-node has at least $k$ nodes from $G$ so that $k$-anonymity is satisfied.

## Algorithm 1: $k$-Anonymity Generalization Algorithm Proposed (Skarkala et al., 2012)

**Input:** graph $G$, parameter $k$
   **Output:** anonymized graph $G'$

1.   **for** each original node $n_i$ **do**
2.   set $sn_i = \{n_i\}$
3.   **end** for
4.   **for** each original edge $e_{i,j}$ **do**
5.   create edge $e_{sni,snj}$
6.   **end** for
7.   **while** (a node $sn_i$ exists such that $|sn_i| < k$) **do**
8.   select a random node $sn_i$ exists such that $|sn_i| < k$
9.   **for** nodes $sn_j$ in *candidates*($sn_i$) **do**
10.  $IL_j = evaluate\_merger(sn_i, sn_j)$
11.  **end** for
12.  choose the node $sn_j$ with the smallest $IL_j$
13.  $merge(sn_i, sn_j)$
14.  **end** while

The codes for the functions in Algorithm 1 is given in Table 1. Function *merger_candidates* is used to add further constraints to the candidate set using three cases. In the first case, it returns a single random supernode from the candidate set. In the second case, the whole set of candidates is returned and in the third case, candidates that are themselves not yet $k$-anonymous are returned.

Skarkala *et al. (2012)* have tested their algorithm on two real weighted undirected graphs namely Karate Club (Zachary, 1977) and Lesmis (Knuth, 1993). Utility of the networks were measured using four structural properties: degree and volume distribution of all nodes in the graph; edge weight

*Table 1. Supporting function codes for Algorithm 1*

| Function *candidates*( $sn_i$ ): | Function *merge*( $sn_i, sn_j$ ): |
|---|---|
| N:= 2-hop neighbors of $sn_i$ <br> **if** (\|N\| > 0) <br> **return** *merger_candidates*(N) <br> **else if** (\|N\| = 0) <br> N:= neighbors of $sn_i$ <br> **if** (\|N\| > 0) <br> **return** *merger_candidates*(N) <br> **else if** (\|N\| = 0) <br> N:= all super-nodes except $sn_i$ <br> **return** *merger_candidates*(N) <br> **end** | Create $sn_{new} := sn_i \cup sn_j$ <br> $N_i :=$ neighbors of $sn_i$ <br> $N_j :=$ neighbors of $sn_j$ <br> **for each** node $n$ in $N_i \cup N_j$ **do** <br> Create edge $e_{n,sn_{new}}$ <br> Compute the weight $w'_{n,sn_{new}}$ <br> Delete edges $e_{n,sn_i}$ and $e_{n,sn_j}$ <br> Delete nodes $sn_i$ and $sn_j$ <br> **end** |
| Function *merger_candidates*(N): <br> **case** *RandomNode*: <br> **return** a random super-node $sn_j \in N$ <br> **case** *AllCandidates*: <br> **return** N <br> **case** *NonAnonymizedCandidates*: <br> **return** $\{sn_j \in N \mid \ \|sn_j\| < k\}$ <br> **end** | Function *evaluate_merger*( $sn_i, sn_j$ ): <br> *merge*( $sn_i, sn_j$ ) <br> compute $IL_j$ for merging $sn_j$ with $sn_i$ <br> undo the merge <br> **return** $IL_j$ <br> **end** |

distribution of all the edges; path length distribution between all pairs of nodes. All the three cases of *merger_candidates* were evaluated upon. In terms of performance time, *RandomNode* is the fastest and *AllCandidates* is the slowest. The degree distribution of both datasets resulted from all three versions and for all *k* parameters were similar to the original. *NonAnonymizedCandidates* version preserves privacy. *AllCandidates* and *NonAnonymizedCandidates* versions preserve three out of four statistical properties in a similar manner.

## k-Anonymous Path Privacy

*k*-anonymous path privacy is an interesting privacy measure applicable to weighted social networks introduced by Wang *et al.* (2011). Shortest paths are a linear property of a social network. The main objective of this type of anonymization is to obfuscate the shortest path between a source node and destination node with *k*-1 other paths so that the true shortest path may not be easily revealed. Consider a small example network shown in Figure 1(a). Suppose the shortest path between nodes 1 and 6 are sensitive and needs to be anonymized. The true shortest path is $\{1 \rightarrow 2 \rightarrow 4 \rightarrow 5\}$. For *k* =2, the proposed algorithm finds the second shortest path reduces proportionally the edge weights of non-overlapping edges between the second shortest and the shortest paths. The anonymized version is shown in Figure 1(b) where the second shortest path $\{1 \rightarrow 2 \rightarrow 3 \rightarrow 6 \rightarrow 5\}$ is altered to have the same cost 8 as in the shortest path by reducing edge (6,5) from 3 to 2 as indicated in bold.

Two algorithms were proposed in Wang et al. (2011). The *k*–single path anonymization algorithm (KSP) is used to anonymize single pair of source and destination vertices. *k*–multi path anonymization algorithm (MSP) is proposed for multiple pairs of source and destination vertices. Note that these algorithms have a main objective to minimally modify the graph structure without adding or deleting any nodes or edges. In order to understand the algorithms, the following notations are to be remembered: $v_i$ (vertex i), $e_{i,j}$ (edge between vertices $v_i$ and $v_j$), $w_{i,j}$ (weight of edge $e_{i,j}$), $p_{i,j}$ (path between vertices $v_i$ and $v_j$), $d_{i,j}$ (length of path $p_{i,j}$), SPL (Shortest Path List) and TSPL (Temporary Shortest Path List)

*Figure 1. k-anonymous path privacy (a)simple network (b) anonymized network with k =2*

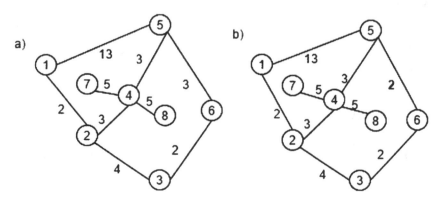

## Algorithm 2: KSP Algorithm (Wang et al. 2011)

**Input:** weighted adjacency matrix $W$ of graph $G$, source and destination vertices for which the shortest path is to be anonymized, parameter $k$
    **Output:** anonymized weight adjacency matrix $W'$

1.     Find the shortest path $p_{i,j}$ and its distance $d_{i,j}$
2.     **for** j from 2 to $k$ **do**
3.     find the j-th shortest path $p'_{i,j}$ and its corresponding length $d'_{i,j}$
4.     **for** each edge $e'_{p,q}$ on $p'_{i,j}$ that is non-overlapping with top (j-1) shortest paths **do**
5.     $w'_{pq} = w'_{pq} + \dfrac{w'_{pq}}{\sum w'_{pq}} \times (d'_{ij} - d_{ij})$
6.     update the adjacency matrix
7.     **end** for
8.     **end** for

## Algorithm 3: MSP Algorithm (Wang et al,, 2011)

**Input:** weighted adjacency matrix $W$ of graph $G$, $H$ which is the set of source and destination vertices for which the shortest path is to be anonymized, parameter $k$
    **Output:** anonymized weight adjacency matrix $W'$

1.     Initialize $SPL = \phi$ //shortest path list
2.     **while** ( $H \neq \phi$ )
3.     **for** each pair of vertices $(v_i, v_j)$ in $H$ **do**
4.     find its shortest path $p_{i,j}$ and corresponding length $d_{i,j}$
5.     **end** for
6.     $d_{r,s} := \min_H (d_{i,j})$ // minimum of all shortest paths
7.     $H := H - \{(v_r, v_s)\}$
8.     $TSPL := \{p_{r,s}\}$ // shortest path for $(v_r, v_s)$
9.     **while** $| TSPL | < k$ **do** // anonymizing $k$ -1 paths
10.     find the next shortest path $p'_{r,s}$ and its corresponding length $d'_{r,s}$
11.     **if** ( $d'_{r,s} = d_{r,s}$ ) **then**
12.     $TSPL := TSPL + p'_{r,s}$ //add to anonymized list if same length

13. **continue**
14. **end** if
15. **else**
16. let $diff := d'_{r,s} - d_{r,s}$
17. $p''_{r,s} := p'_{r,s} - \{$edges in SPL and TSPL$\}$
18. **if** ($p''_{r,s} \neq \phi$ and $d''_{r,s} > diff$) **then** // available edges
19. **for** each edge $e''_{i,j}$ on path $p''_{r,s}$ **do**
20. $w''_{i,j} = w''_{i,j} + \dfrac{w''_{i,j}}{\sum w''_{i,j}} \times (d'_{r,s} - diff)$
21. update the adjacency matrix
22. $TSPL := TSPL + p'_{r,s}$
23. **end** for
24. **end** if
25. **end** else
26. **end** while
27. $SPL := SPL + TSPL$
28. **end** while

## ($k_1$, $k_2$)-Shortest Path Privacy

One major drawback of $k$-anonymous path privacy is that it does not consider degree attacks on the anonymized shortest paths. Therefore, if an adversary has background knowledge of node degrees on the shortest path, the true shortest path can be identified even after anonymization. In order to combat this effect, Wang *et al.* modified their algorithm and proposed a new concept called ($k_1$, $k_2$)-shortest path privacy (Wang et al, 2013). A network satisfies ($k_1$, $k_2$)-shortest path privacy if it not only has at least $k_1$ indistinguishable shortest paths between the source and destination vertices but for the non-overlapping vertices on the $k_1$ shortest paths, there exist at least $k_2$ vertices with same node degree and lie on more than one shortest path. By proposing this condition, an adversary cannot estimate the shortest path with ease even if background degree information of the vertices is available. To understand better, consider the network shown in Figure 1(a). If the adversary knows that the shortest path contains a vertex with degree 4 then the shortest path $\{1 \rightarrow 2 \rightarrow 4 \rightarrow 5\}$ can be identified because vertex 4 is the only vertex with a degree of 4.

The proposed algorithm works in 2 phases. The first phase is similar to the $k$-anonymous path privacy algorithm where the objective is to modify the weights of the top $k_1$ shortest paths so that all have the same length. The second phase is to find groups of $k_2$ vertices that are not on the same $k_1$ shortest paths, and adding edges to these vertices so that they will have same vertex degrees. Three simple clustering strategies namely modified $k$-means clustering, sorting and dynamic programming methods have been considered to satisfy the second phase. In the algorithm, $TN$ indicates the non-overlapping vertices on shortest paths, $SP$ denotes the shortest path and $NSP$ indicates the vertices on the shortest path. Each of the three algorithms given below take the input graph $G$, source vertex $V_s$, destination vertex $V_d$ and parameters $(k_1, k_2)$ as input. The algorithm outputs clusters of vertices that should be anonymized with the same vertex degree.

## Algorithm 4: (k1, k2)-Shortest Path Privacy Algorithm

### *Modified k-Means Clustering Algorithm*

1. Find all $SPs$ and $N_{SP}$
2. Let $TN = \{ t_i \mid$ the set of all transfer nodes$\} = N_{sp} - \{V_s, V_d\}$
3. **if** $|TN| < 2k_2$ **then**
4. there exists only one cluster
5. **end** if
6. $K = \left\lceil \dfrac{|TN|}{k_2} \right\rceil$
5. Randomly pick K nodes as initial clusters
6. **while** centroid of clusters remains constant **do**
7. Form K clusters by assigning each point to the closest centroid
8. Re-assign clusters such that each cluster has size $k_2 \leq |C_i| \leq 2k_2 - 1$
9. Re-compute centroid of each cluster
10. **end** while

### *Sorting-Based Clustering Algorithm*

1. Find all $SPs$ and $N_{SP}$
2. Let $TN = \{ t_i \mid$ the set of all transfer nodes$\}$
3. Sort $TN$ in descending order according to node degree

4. **while** $|TN| \neq 0$ **or** $|TN| > (2k\text{-}1)$ **do**
5. move first $k_2$ nodes into the distinct group
6. **end** while
7. **if** $|TN| \neq 0$ **then**
8. Move the remaining nodes into a group

### Dynamic Programming-Based Algorithm

1. Find all $SPs$ and $N_{SP}$
2. Let $TN = \{ t_i \mid$ the set of all transfer nodes$\}$
3. Sort $TN$ in descending order according to node degree
4. Let $I(d[i,j]) = \sum_{i=1}^{j}(d_i - d_j)$
5. **if** $\left|TN\right| < 2k_2$ **then**
6. $D_A(d[1,i]) = I(d[1,i])$
7. **else**
8. $D_A(d[1,i]) = \min_{\max(k_2.i-2k_2+1)\leq t\leq i-k_2}\left\{D_A(d[1,t]) + I(d[t+1,i])\right\}$
9. **end** if-else

Experiments conducted in Wang et al. (2013) indicate that simple sorting-based technique requires addition of relatively few edges compared to the other two approaches. Simple sorting based approach also yields average clustering co-efficients and average shortest path lengths closer to the original graph. These results indicate that simple sorting-based technique is a simple and efficient method to achieve $(k_1, k_2)$-shortest path privacy.

# DIRECTED WEIGHTED SOCIAL NETWORKS

## k-Anonymous Path Privacy

Tsai *et al.* (2012) proposed a new algorithm to achieve *k*-anonymous path privacy by using a greedy approach that considers two types of edges namely Partially-Visited ($PV$) edges and None-Visited ($NV$) edges. The graph $G$ is considered to have three types of edges. An edge is a $PV$ edge if one path passes through this edge, which is on the specific shortest path, but not all shortest paths in $H$ which is the set of source and destination vertices. The

*PV* edges can only be modified one time. An edge is an *AV* edge if all shortest paths (including modified) from all pairs of source and destination vertices pass through this edge. The modified paths, which are not shortest paths, also need to pass through. An edge is a *NV* edge if the edge doesn't belong to any shortest paths or modified paths.

Consider a weighted directed graph shown in Figure 2 (a). Let there be two shortest sensitive paths in $H$, given by $SP_1$ and $SP_2$. $SP_1$ is between $v_1$ and $v_6$ where the shortest path is given by $\{(v_1, v_2), (v_2, v_5), (v_5, v_6)\}$ and $SP_2$ is between $v_4$ and $v_6$ where the shortest path is given by $\{(v_4, v_5), (v_5, v_6)\}$. In the graph, all edges are *PV* edges which are passed through by $SP_1$ or $SP_2$ such as $(v_1, v_2), (v_2, v_5), (v_4, v_5)$ and $(v_5, v_6)$ in the initial stage. *AV* edge is the edge through which both the shortest paths $SP_1$ and $SP_2$ pass through such as $(v_5, v_6)$ in the initial stage. *NV* edges are the edges not in the shortest path such as $(v_1, v_3), (v_2, v_3), (v_3, v_5)$ and so on. To achieve 2-anonymous path privacy on $SP_1$ and $SP_2$ for $P_{11} = \{(v_1, v_3), (v_3, v_5), (v_5, v_6)\}$ in $SP_1$ we need to modify the weights of edges $e_{1,3}$ to 4.5 and $e_{3,5}$ to 6.5 so that it has the same shortest path length. For $SP_2$, if the path lengths of $SP_1$ have been modified then $P_{21} = \{(v_4, v_3), (v_3, v_5), (v_5, v_6)\}$ where the new path length is 22.5, only weight of edge $e_{4,3}$ needs to be modified to 3.5. The anonymized graph is shown in Figure 2(b).

The algorithms used in this section use weighed-proportional-based strategy to modify the weights of edges which states that the weights for the

*Figure 2. k-anonymous path privacy on weighted directed networks (a) simple network (b) anonymized network with k =2*
*Tsai et al., 2012.*

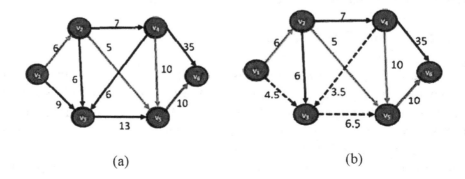

(a)                                         (b)

modified edges may not only be decreased but can also be increased to achieve the $k$-shortest paths. In addition, the modified edges of each path might be overlapped and required to have the cyclic check (Wang et al., 2011). In order to minimize the changes of weight, if more edges are modified, it may have less influence on the original graph. Based on this idea, PV and NV edges are selected first for anonymization. Note that modifying PV weights has 2 side effects that need to be considered. Firstly, the path length of the selected sensitive shortest path might be reduced. Secondly, new shortest path might be shorter than original shortest path. To combat the first side-effect, each PV edge, which the selected sensitive shortest path passes through, can only be modified one time. This avoids too much influence on anonymized paths. To combat the second side-effect, we allow the edge weights not only to be decreased but also to be increased.

## Algorithm 5: k-Multiple Paths Anonymization on PV+NV (KMPPN)

**Input:** $W$ which is the weighted adjacency matrix of graph $G$, $H$ which is the set of source and destination vertices to be anonymized and parameter $k$.

   **Output:** anonymized weighted adjacency matrix $W^*$

1.   Initialize $SPL = \phi$ //shortest path list
2.   **while** $H \neq \phi$ **do**
3.   **for** each pair of vertices $(v_i, v_j)$ in $H$ **do**
4.   find the shortest path $p_{i,j}$ and length $d_{i,j}$
5.   **end** for
6.   $d_{r,s} = \min_H d_{i,j}$ // the minimum of all shortest paths
7.   $H := H - (v_r, v_s)$
8.   $TSPL := \{p_{r,s}\}$ // save the shortest path for $(v_r, v_s)$
9.   **while** $|TSPL| < k$ **do** // happens when there are less than $k$ paths for current vertex pair
10.  find the next shortest path $p'_{r,s}$ and length $d'_{r,s}$
11.  **if** $d'_{r,s} = d_{r,s}$ **then** // having same length
12.  $TSPL := TSPL + p'_{r,s}$ // add to anonymized list
13.  **continue** // to find the next shortest path
14.  **else** // having different length

15. **if** $d'_{r,s}$ and $d_{r,s}$ satisfy cyclic check **then**

16. **continue** // $d'_{r,s}$ can't be anonymized

17. **end** if

16. $diff = d'_{r,s} - d_{r,s}$ // weight to be reduced

17. $PV\_NV\_\mathrm{Pr}ocess(p'_{r,s}, diff)$ // calls a procedure

18. **end** if-else

19. **end** while

20. $SPL := SPL + TSPL$

21. **end** while

The pseudo-code for the function $PV\_NV\_Process$ is given below:

$PV\_NV\_Process(p'_{r,s}, diff)$

1. $p''_{r,s} := p'_{r,s}$ - {edges in $SPL$ and $TSPL$ } // consider only $NV$ edges

2. $p''_{r,s} := p''_{r,s}$ + {edges which appeared in $p_{i,j}$ and never modified} // this considers $PV$ edges

3. **if** $p''_{r,s} \neq \phi$ **then** // there exists edges to be modified

4. **for** each edge $e''_{i,j}$ on the $p''_{r,s}$ **do**

5. $w''_{i,j} = w''_{i,j} - \dfrac{w''_{i,j}}{\sum w''_{i,j}} \times diff$

6. update the adjacency matrix

7. $TSPL := TSPL + p'_{r,s}$ // save the modified path

8. **end** for

9. **for** each $PV$ edge $e'''_{i,j}$ on $p''_{r,s}$ **do**

10. $PVdiff = PVdiff + (w''_{i,j} - w'''_{i,j})$ // weights of $PV$ to be reduced

11. **end** for

12. **if** $PVdiff > 0$ **then**

13. **for** each $NV$ edge $e''''_{i,j}$ on path $p'''_{r,s}$ in $(TSPL\_SPL - H)$ **do**

14. $w''''_{i,j} = w''''_{i,j} - \dfrac{w''''_{i,j}}{\sum w''''_{i,j}} \times PVdiff$

15. **end** for

16. **end** if

17. **end** if

The KMPNN algorithm suffers from a side effect where the path length of selected sensitive shortest paths is reduced. The second algorithm proposed in Tsai et al (2012) is the *k*-Multiple Paths Anonymization on *NV*

algorithm (*KMPNN*), which not only modifies the *NV* edges, but also minimizes the change of edges weights on selected sensitive shortest paths. Function $PV\_NV\_Process$ is replaced by $NV\_Process$ whose pseudo-code is given below:

$NV\_Process$

1.  $p''_{r,s} := p'_{r,s}$ - {edges in $SPL$ and $TSPL$ } // consider only $NV$ edges
2.  **if** $p''_{r,s} \neq \phi$ **then** // there exists edges to be modified
3.  **for** each edge $e''_{i,j}$ on $p''_{r,s} \neq \phi$ **do** // reduce proportionality
4.  $w'''_{i,j} = w''_{i,j} - \dfrac{w''_{i,j}}{\sum w''_{i,j}} \times diff$
5.  update the adjacency matrix
6.  $TSPL := TSPL + p'_{r,s}$ // save the modified path
7.  **end** for
8.  **end** if

# CONVERTING DIRECTED NETWORKS INTO UNDIRECTED NETWORKS

In this section, we will look at an interesting transformation approach that is used mainly to cluster directed networks by first transforming them into undirected networks and then applying any of the clustering techniques proposed for undirected networks. The directionality information is incorporated using weights on the edges of the transformed network. Let $G$ be the directed graph and $M$ it's adjacency matrix. The following symmetrization methods can be applied:

1.  ***M+M^T* Symmetrization:** In this method, the resultant undirected graph $G_U$ has the adjacency matrix $M_U = M + M^T$. From the resultant adjacency matrix, we can observe that this method ignores the

directionality in-case of only one directional edge between a pair of nodes and sums the weight of the edges if there exist directional edges in both directions between a pair of nodes.

2.   **Random Walk Symmetrization:** Let $P$ be the transition matrix of the random walk which can be obtained by normalizing the rows of input adjacency matrix $M$. The resultant transformed graph will be represented by the adjacency matrix $M_U = \dfrac{\Pi P + P^T \Pi}{2}$ where $\Pi$ is the diagonal of $\pi_1, \pi_2, ..., \pi_n$ which are the probabilities of staying at each node in the stationary state. This can be obtained via power iterations. For the symmetric matrix $G_U$ obtained using this adjacency matrix $M_U$, the undirected normalized cut on this graph is equal to the directed normalized cut on the original directed graph, for any subset of vertices $S$. Note that this symmetrization has the exact same number of edges as the previous approach because $P$ and $P^T$ have the same non-zero structure as $A$ and $A^T$. Also, $\Pi$ is the diagonal matrix. But the weights assigned to the edges will be different from the previous approach.

# LINEAR PROPERTY PRESERVING ANONYMIZATION APPROACH

We will look at an anonymization technique that seeks to preserve the linear property of the weighted network while anonymization. A linear property of a graph is a property expressible in terms of inequalities involving linear combination of edge weights. Examples of linear property in graphs include graph clustering, shortest paths, spanning tree, maximizing information spread and so on. Das *et al. (2009)* have considered shortest paths problem as a primary linear property to be preserved as it forms the basis for a number of other graph properties. The edge neighborhood of a vertex $u$ denoted by $N_u$ is the set of edges which have $u$ as the source. The definition of k-anonymity considered is different this context of weighted edges. An edge $(u, v)$ is considered to be k-anonymous if there are k-1 other edges $(u, v')$ in $N_u$ such that $|| w[u, v] - w[u, v'] || \leq \mu$ where $\mu$ is the indistinguishability threshold(the difference of weights below which two edge weights cannot be distinguished).

# Dijkstra's Algorithm

Dijkstra's algorithm is a widely used greedy algorithm for finding the single source shortest path tree. We will first describe this algorithm and then look at the linear complexity model proposed in Das et al. (2009). Taking a start vertex as $v_0$, Dijkstra algorithm selects the vertex $u$ with the minimum cost from $v_0$. Then, the algorithm tries to relax the neighbors of $u$ by checking to see if the cost from the start vertex has decreased by selecting $u$. Thus, the algorithm makes a decision when to relax a neighbor and which vertex to choose for the next iteration. The pseudocode is given by Algorithm 6 below:

## Algorithm 6: Dijkstra Algorithm

**Input:** Directed weighted graph $G = (V, E, W)$, start vertex $v_0$.
    **Output:** Shortest paths tree rooted at the start vertex $v_0$.

1.    $D \leftarrow (\infty)$ (Cost of best known path from source taken as infinity initially)
2.    $\Pi \leftarrow ()$ (Predecessor in shortest path from source)
3.    $Q \leftarrow v_0$ (Set of unvisited vertices)
4.    $S \leftarrow \phi$ (Vertices to which shortest path is known)
5.    $D[v_0, v_0] \leftarrow 0$
6.    **while** $Q \neq \phi$ **do**
7.    $u \leftarrow \text{ExtractMin}(Q)$ (The unvisited vertex with minimum cost)
8.    $S \leftarrow S \cup \{u\}$
9.    **for** each vertex $v$ such that $(u, v) \in E$ and $v \notin S$ **do**
10.   **if** $D[v_0, v] > D[v_0, u] + w[u, v]$ **then**
11.   $D[v_0, v] \leftarrow D[v_0, u] + w[u, v]$
12.   $\Pi(v) \leftarrow u$ (Shorter path exists)
13.   **else**
14.   (Do nothing here)
15.   **end if-else**
16.   **if** $v \notin Q$ **then**
17.   $Q \leftarrow Q \cup \{v\}$
18.   **end if**
19.   **end for**
20.   **end while**

## Linear Complexity Model

Dijkstra's algorithm makes many decisions based on the outcome of comparisons of linear combination of edge weights. These decisions can be modelled using three categories of inequalities. There inequalities incorporated into the Dijkstra's algorithm gives us the linear complexity model. The pseudocode is given in Algorithm 7. Remember that $D[u,v]$ is the cost of path from vertex $u$ to vertex $v$. In the algorithm, $x_{(u,v)}$ is the variable corresponding to edge $(u,v) \in E$, $P[u,v]$ is the path from vertex $u$ to vertex $v$ and $f(u,v) = \sum\limits_{(u',v') \in P[u,v]} x_{(u',v')}$ which is the sum of the path in terms of variables representing the edges in the graph. The three categories are:

**Category 1:** When processing an edge $(u,v)$, if $D[v_0,v]$ can be improved then $D[v_0,v] > D[v_0,u] + w[u,v]$ and add constraint that $f(v_0,v) > f(v_0,u) + x_{(u,v)}$. (This category is incorporated in Line 18 of Algorithm 7).

**Category 2:** When processing an edge $(u,v)$, if $D[v_0,v]$ cannot be improved then $D[v_0,v] < D[v_0,u] + w[u,v]$ and add constraint that $f(v_0,v) \leq f(v_0,u) + x_{(u,v)}$. (This category is incorporated in Line 20 of Algorithm 7).

**Category 3:** When extracting the edge $u$ for the next iteration, if $u'$ was the previous vertex processed, then $D[v_0,u'] \leq D[v_0,u]$ and add constraint $f(v_0,u') \leq f(v_0,u)$ which helps to capture the order in which the vertices are selected. (This category is incorporated in Line 11 of Algorithm 7).

## Algorithm 7. Linear Complexity Model

**Input:** Directed weighted graph $G = (V,E,W)$, start vertex $v_0$.

**Output:** Shortest paths tree rooted at the start vertex $v_0$. Any solution to the model used to anonymize edge weights in the graph will result in the same shortest paths tree in the original as well as the anonymized graph.

1.  $D \leftarrow (\infty)$ (Cost of best known path from source taken as infinity initially)
2.  $\Pi \leftarrow ()$ (Predecessor in shortest path from source)
3.  $Q \leftarrow v_0$ (Set of unvisited vertices)

4.    $S \leftarrow \phi$ (Vertices to which shortest path is known)

5.    $D[v_0, v_0] \leftarrow 0$

6.    $u' \leftarrow \phi$ (Stores the vertex processed in previous iteration)

7.    **while** $Q \neq \phi$ **do**

8.    $u \leftarrow$ ExtractMin($Q$) (The unvisited vertex with minimum cost)

9.    $S \leftarrow S \cup \{u\}$

10.  **if** $u' \neq \phi$ **then**

11.  AddConstraint($f(v_0, u') \leq f(v_0, u)$)

12.  **end if**

13.  $u' \leftarrow u$

14.  **for** each vertex $v$ such that $(u, v) \in E$ and $v \notin S$ **do**

15.  **if** $D[v_0, v] > D[v_0, u] + w[u, v]$ **then**

16.  $D[v_0, v] \leftarrow D[v_0, u] + w[u, v]$

17.  $\Pi(v) \leftarrow u$ (Shorter path exists)

18.  AddConstraint($f(v_0, v) > f(v_0, u) + x_{(u,v)}$)

19.  **else**

20.  AddConstraint($f(v_0, v) \leq f(v_0, u) + x_{(u,v)}$)

21.  **end if-else**

22.  **if** $v \notin Q$ **then**

23.  $Q \leftarrow Q \cup \{v\}$

24.  **end if**

25.  **end for**

26.  **end while**

As for complexity, categories 1 and 2 combined result in $O(dn)$ inequalities where $d$ is the average degree per node and category 3 has $O(n)$ inequalities.

## Reduced Model

Das *et al. (2009)* also proposed a model with reduced complexity as the linear model. It is based on the principle that it does not matter how many times the cost of the path to a particular vertex is improved, the minimum among these costs determine the shortest path from source. Category 3 models this information efficiently, so this model only uses category 3. The pseudocode of this model is given in Algorithm 8 below:

## Algorithm 8: Reduced Complexity Model

**Input:** Directed weighted graph $G = (V, E, W)$, start vertex $v_0$.

**Output:** Shortest paths tree rooted at the start vertex $v_0$ modelled using only category 3.

1.  $D \leftarrow (\infty)$ (Cost of best known path from source taken as infinity initially)
2.  $\Pi \leftarrow ()$ (Predecessor in shortest path from source)
3.  $Q \leftarrow v_0$ (Set of unvisited vertices)
4.  $S \leftarrow \phi$ (Vertices to which shortest path is known)
5.  $D[v_0, v_0] \leftarrow 0$
6.  $T \leftarrow \phi$ (Set of edges in the tree)
7.  **while** $Q \neq \phi$ **do**
8.  $u \leftarrow \text{ExtractMin}(Q)$ (The unvisited vertex with minimum cost)
9.  $S \leftarrow S \cup \{u\}$
10. **if** $(\Pi(u), u) \notin T$ **then**
11. $T \leftarrow T \cup (\Pi(u), u)$
12. **end if**
13. **if** $u' \neq \phi$ **then**
14. $\text{AddConstraint}(f(v_0, u') \leq f(v_0, u))$
15. **end if**
16. $u' \leftarrow u$
17. **for** each vertex $v$ such that $(u, v) \in E$ and $v \notin S$ **do**
18. **if** $D[v_0, v] > D[v_0, u] + w[u, v]$ **then**
19. $D[v_0, v] \leftarrow D[v_0, u] + w[u, v]$
20. $\Pi(v) \leftarrow u$ (Shorter path exists)
21. **else**
22. (Do nothing here)
23. **end if-else**
24. **if** $v \notin Q$ **then**
25. $Q \leftarrow Q \cup \{v\}$
26. **end if**
27. **end for**
28. **end while**

Note that category 3 only considers edges which are part of the shortest paths tree. No constraints are put on non-tree edges which can lead to a violation in the order of the anonymized graph. To add non-tree edges into the constraints of the model $\forall (u,v) \in E \wedge (u,v) \notin T_s$, we $AddConstraint \left( x_{(u,v)} > f(v_s, v_l) \right)$ where $v_l$ is the last vertex processed by Dijkstra's Algorithm and $T_s$ is the shortest path tree obtained as output from the algorithm. Algorithm 8 has a complexity of $O(n-1)$ and Algorithm 9 described below is one possible scheme for weight reassignment.

## Algorithm 9: Reassignment of Weights in Reduced Model

**Require:** $v_l$ which is the last vertex processed in Algorithm 8.

1.   **for** each edge $(u,v) \in E$ **do**
2.   **if** $(u,v) \in T$ **then**
3.   $w'[u,v] \leftarrow$ Value obtained from the solution of model.
4.   **else**
5.   $w'[u,v] \leftarrow D'[v_s, v_l] + rand()$ ( $v_s$ is the source vertex)
6.   **end if-else**
7.   **end for**

## CONCLUSION

Graphs can be weighted, directed or both. Many social networks fall under this category. In this chapter we first discussed on weighted social networks. Under this we considered the general approach, k-anonymous path privacy and (k1, k2)- shortest path privacy. Similarly, we also discussed on directed weighted social networks and anonymisation techniques for these type of social networks. Here also, we discussed upon k-anonymous path privacy. If directed networks can be converted to an equivalent undirected network then the existing algorithms for undirected networks can be applied to solve the anonymisation problems for them. Techniques for such a transformation are provided here. In anonymisation of social networks one of the desirable constraints is the preservation of properties of the original network as far as practicable. We discussed here an anonymisation approach for preservation of linear property.

# REFERENCES

Das, S., Egecioglu, O., & Abbadi, A. E. (2009). *Anonymizing edge-weighted social network graphs, Technical report*. UCSB CS.

Knuth, D. E. (1993). *The Stanford Graph Base: A platform for Combinatorial Computing*. Reading, MA: Addison-Wesley.

Skarkala, M., Maragoudakis, M., Gritzalis, S., Mitrou, L., Toivonen, H., & Moen, P. (2012). Privacy Preservation by K-Anonymization of weighted Social Networks. IEEE Computer Society, ASONAM, 423-428. doi:10.1109/ASONAM.2012.75

Tsai, Y., Wang, S., Kao, H., & Hong, T. (2012). Confining edge types in k-anonymization of shortest paths. *Proceedings on the Third IEEE International Conference on Innovations in Bio-Inspired Computing and Applications (IBICA)*, 318-322. doi:10.1109/IBICA.2012.18

Wang, S. L., Shih, C. C., Ting, H. H., & Hong, T. P. (2013). Degree anonymization for K-shortest-path privacy. In *Proceedings on the IEEE international conference on Systems, Man, and Cybernetics*. Manchester, UK: IEEE. doi:10.1109/SMC.2013.190

Wang, S. L., Tsai, Z. Z., Hong, T. P., & Ting, H. H. (2011). Anonymizing Shortest Paths on Social Network Graphs. *Proceedings on The Third Asian Conference on Intelligent Information and Database Systems*. doi:10.1007/978-3-642-20039-7_13

Zachary, W. (1977). An information flow model for conflict and fission in small groups. *Journal of Anthropological Research, 33*(4), 452–473. doi:10.1086/jar.33.4.3629752

Chapter 7
# De–Anonymization Techniques

## ABSTRACT

*Most operators provide some privacy controls such that many online networks restrict access to the information about individual members and their relationships. In a paper in 2006, it is claimed that the authors have developed a two-stage de-anonymisation algorithm that can re-identify the original network from an anonymised network obtained by using any of the anonymization algorithms developed thus far. However, at that time anonymisation, techniques for social networks were in their infancy. Several powerful anonymisation algorithms have been developed after that as explained in the previous chapters. But it seems that anonymisation algorithms and de-anonymisation algorithms have been developed alternatively. The authors present some more de-anonymisation algorithms developed subsequently, as late as 2017.*

## INTRODUCTION

As we have seen in the previous chapters, preserving privacy of respondents in a social network before publishing has become of utmost importance. Even in online networks that are completely open, there is a disconnection between users' willingness to share information and their reaction to unintended parties viewing or using their information (Carthy, 2007). As a consequence, most operators provide some privacy controls such that many online networks restrict access to the information about individual members and their relationships.

DOI: 10.4018/978-1-5225-5158-4.ch007

But, the network owners share the information with advertising partners and third parties. More often than not the published networks are used for research purposes. So, as discussed earlier the networks are anonymised before publication. It has been interpreted that anonymity is equivalent to privacy in several high-profile cases of data sharing.

In Narayanan and Shmatikov (2009), which they claim to be the first paper in their direction, it is demonstrated as how it is feasible to de-anonymise real world social networks. For this purpose the following steps have been taken out.

- A survey of the current state of data sharing in social networks, the purpose of such sharing, the resulting privacy risks and the availability of auxiliary information, which an attacker can use for de-anonymisation, is made.
- Privacy in social networks and its relation to node anonymity is defined formally. A categorization of attackers basing upon categories of attack determined through differentiation of attackers' resources and auxiliary information is made. A methodology for measuring the extent of privacy breaches in social networks is provided.
- Most importantly, a generic re-identification algorithm for anonymised social networks is developed. The algorithm uses only the network structure and does not make any additional assumptions about membership overlap between multiple networks. An illustration of the functionality of the algorithm is explained by taking two large real-worlds online social networks; Flickr and Twitter.

We have discussed in the beginning and other chapters before that publishing social networks is necessary for different purposes and the owners are willingly or compelled by the situation intend to publish such networks. The various reasons for such inclination are:

## Academic and Government Data Mining

Phone call networks are commonly used to detect illicit activity such as calling fraud and for national security purposes. Sociologists, epidemiologists and health-care professionals collect data about geographic, friendship, family networks to study disease propagation and risk. Even when obtained from public websites, if it is released still presents privacy risks as the attackers who do not have resources can use it. Of course sometimes pseudo anonymised profiles are provided, which are similar to anonymised network.

## Advertising

As social network data makes commerce much more profitable, network operators are inclined to share their graphs with advertising partners to enable better social targeting for advertisements. As an example Facebook explicitly says that users' profiles may be shared for the purpose of personalizing advertisements and promotions as long as the individual is not explicitly identified (Facebook, 2007).

## Third-Party Applications

Although third-party applications do not respect privacy policies, the data provided to third-party applications is usually not anonymised, even though most applications would be able to function on anonymised profiles. So, data from multiple applications can be aggregated and used for targeted advertising. It has been observed that a malicious third-party application can learn about members of a social network even if it obtains the data in anonymised form.

## Aggregation

Aggregation of information from multiple social networks potentially presents a greater threat to individual privacy than one-time data releases. Aggregated networks are an excellent source of auxiliary information for attacks.

## Other Data-Release Scenarios

There are other organisations like the WellNet health care coordination service, "friend-to-friend networking" which also insist on data anonymisation of their networks before release. Photographs published online without identifying information help in identifying faces as users who appear together in photographs are likely to be neighbours in the social network.

# DE-ANONYMISATION ATTACKS

Two types of active attacks are proposed in Backstrom et al. (2007) and Guha, Tang, and Francis (2008), which deal with edge privacy in anonymised social networks. The basic assumption in such attacks is that the adversary is able to modify the network prior to its release. An adversary chooses an arbitrary set of users whose privacy it wishes to violate, creates a small number of new user accounts with edges to these targeted users and creates a pattern of links among the new accounts with the goal of making it stands out in the anonymised graph structure. The attacker creates O(log N) Sybil nodes, whose outgoing edges help re-identify nodes.

But active attacks are difficult to apply on a large scale. Moreover, these are restricted to online social networks.

The attacker has little control over the edges incoming to the nodes he creates as the legitimate users will not have interest or opportunity to connect to Sybil nodes. It has been observed in Narayanan and Shmatikov (2009) this property may enable the network operator to recognise that the network has been compromised by a Sybil attack.

The third limitation is active attacks is the fact that many online social networks require a link to be mutual before the information is made available in any form. Thus, with the assumption as mentioned in the previous paragraph, the links from fake nodes to real ones do not show up in the network. Also, large-scale active attacks require a huge number of Sybil nodes, which is not feasible practically.

In Guha, Tang, and Francis (2008), the notion of passive attacks was also considered. In such attacks, a small coalition of users discovers their location in the anonymised graph by utilising the knowledge of the network structure around them. This attack is plausible but can be applied to small networks only.

In contrast, the algorithm proposed in Narayanan and Shmatikov (2009) does not require the creation of a large number of Sybil nodes. It can be used for reasonably large social networks.

It has been claimed by the authors, existing privacy protection mechanics for social networks are only effective against very restricted adversaries and have been evaluated on small, simulated networks whose characteristics are different from real social networks. As an example they have cited that the approach by Zheleva and Getoor (2007) ignores auxiliary information that may be available to the attacker. In some other approaches like in Guha et al

(2008) and Hay et al. (2007), use the idea which depend upon a more sound architecture based upon server-side Facebook application.

Anonymity is a popular approach to protect privacy. Felt and Evans (2008) propose a system where applications see randomised tokens representing users instead of actual identifiers. Frikken and Golle (2006) show how to compute an anonymous graph from pieces held by different participants in order to perform privacy-preserving social network analysis.

Hay et al (2007) require nodes to be automatically equivalent; that is there must exist auto morphisms of the graph that map each of k nodes to one another, which is an extremely strong structural requirement, which is achieved only against severely restricted adversaries. Zhou and Pei (2008) assume that the adversary knows the exact 1-neighbourhood of the target node. The anonymisation algorithm attempts to make this 1-neighbourhood isomorphic to k-1 other 1-neighbourhoods via edge addition. However, the edge addition requires a good percentage of the existing nodes and if the average degree of nodes increases this number is likely to rise sharply.

The conclusions drawn in Narayanan and Shmatikov (2009) are as follows:

The fundamental problem with k-anonymity is that it is a syntactic property which may not provide any privacy even when satisfied.

Also, these algorithms impose arbitrary restrictions on the information available to the adversaries and make arbitrary assumptions about the properties of the social network

Auxiliary information which is likely to be available to the attacker is global in nature and not restricted to the neighbourhood of a single node.

Thus they tried to develop an algorithm which can use auxiliary information available to the attacker can be used for re-identification of some nodes even for noisy information. Once some re-identification of a few nodes are made it provides more auxiliary information for further re-identification.

## TWO STAGE DE-ANONYMISATION ALGORITHM (NARAYANA & SSHMATIKOV, 2009)

The proposed algorithm runs in two stages.

**Stage 1:** The attacker identifies a small number of "seed" nodes which are present both in the anonymous target graph and the attacker's auxiliary graph and maps them to each other.

**Stage 2:** It is a self-reinforcing process in which the seed mapping is extended to new nodes using only the topology of the network and the new mapping is fed back to the algorithm.

The eventual result is a large mapping between subgraphs of the auxiliary and target networks which re-identifies all mapped nodes in the later.

## Seed Identification

A possible seed identification algorithm is described here. Another such algorithm is described in Narayanan and Shmatikov (2009). The basic assumption is that the attacker's individual auxiliary information consists of a clique of k nodes which are present both in the auxiliary and the target graphs. It is sufficient to know the degree of each of these nodes and the number of common neighbours for each pair of nodes.

Inputs:

1.    The target graph
2.    k seed nodes in the auxiliary graph
3.    k node-degree values
4.    $\binom{k}{2}$ pairs of common-neighbour counts
5.    Error parameter $\varepsilon$

## Procedure

The algorithm searches the target graph for a unique k-clique with matching node degrees and common-neighbour counts. If found the algorithm maps the nodes in the clique to the corresponding nodes in the auxiliary graph, otherwise failure is reported.

The above procedure seems to be a brute-force search and is exponential in k. However, in practice it does not create any problem due to;

1.    If the degree is bounded by d, then the complexity is $O(n.d^{k-1})$.
2.    The running time is heavily input-dependent and the inputs with high running time turn out to produce a large number of matches.
3.    Terminating the algorithm as soon as more than one match is found greatly decreases the running time.

## Propagation

**Input:** Two graphs $G_1 = (V_1, E_1)$ and $G_2 = (V_2, E_2)$; a partial "seed" mapping $\mu_S$ between the two.

**Output:** A mapping $\mu$

Although probabilistic mappings may be thought of, finding a one-one mapping $\mu$ has been found to be simpler.

## Procedure

The algorithm finds a new mapping using the topological structure of the network and the feedback from previously constructed mappings. It is robust to mild modifications of the topology such as those introduced by sanitization.

At each iteration the algorithm starts with the accumulated list of mapped pairs between $V_1$ and $V_2$. It picks an arbitrary unmapped node u in $V_1$ and computes a score for each unmapped node v in $V_2$, equal to the number of neighbours of u that have been mapped to neighbours of v. If the strength of the match is above a threshold, the mapping between u and v is added to the list and the next iteration starts.

## Some Concepts

The following concepts are used in the context of the algorithm.

- **Eccentricity:** It is a heuristic defined in Narayanan and Shmatikov (2009) in the context of de-anonymising databases. It measures how much an item in a set X "stands out" from the rest and is defined as

$$\frac{\max(X) - \max_2(X)}{\sigma(X)}$$

where max and $\max_2$ denote the highest and second highest values, respectively and $\sigma$ denotes the standard deviation.

In the two phase algorithm, the eccentricity is measured for the set of mapping scores and rejects the match if the eccentricity score is below a certain threshold.

- **Edge Directionality:** Since directed graphs are considered n this algorithm, to compute the mapping score between a pair of nodes u and v, the algorithm computes two scores; the first one is based only on the incoming edges of u and v and the second one based only on the outgoing edges. These two scores are then summed.

- **Node Degrees:** The score as computed above are biased towards the nodes with high degrees. So in order to compensate this, the score of each node is divided by the square root of its degree.

- **Revisiting Nodes:** At the early stages of the algorithm, there are a few mappings to work with and therefore the algorithm makes more errors. As the algorithm progresses, the number of mapped nodes increases and the error rate goes down. Thus the need to revisit already mapped nodes, the mapping computed when revisiting a node may be different because of the new mappings that have become available.

- **Reverse Match:** The algorithm is completely un consequential about the semantics of the two graphs. It does not matter whether $G_1$ is the target graph and $G_2$ is the auxiliary graph or the other way it is true. Each time a node u maps to v, the mapping scores are computed with the input graphs switched. If v gets mapped back to u, the mapping is retained; otherwise it is rejected.

The complexity of the algorithm is $O(|E_1|d_2)$, where $d_2$ is abound on the degree of the nodes in $V_2$ if we ignore revisiting nodes and reverse matches. Assuming that a node is revisited only if the number of already-mapped neighbours of the node has increased by at least 1, we get a bound of $O(|E_1|d_1.d_2)$, where $d_1$ is a bound on the degree of the nodes in $V_1$. Finally, taking reverse mapping into account the complexity becomes $O((|E_1|+|E_2|)d_1.d_2)$.

This algorithm specifies that anonymity is not sufficient for privacy when dealing with social networks. The generic re-identification algorithm can successfully de-anonymize several thousand users in the anonymous graph of a popular microblogging services. Also, the feasibility of a successful re-identification is demonstrated based on the network topology and assuming that the target graph is completely anonymised. In practice, anonymised graphs are released with at least some attributes in their nodes and edges, making de-anonymisation further easier.

# OTHER DE-ANONYMISATION TECHNIQUES

In Peng et al (2014), it is shown that using a divide and conquer approach to strengthen the power of the de-anonymisation algorithms can be further strengthened. Their approach partitions the networks into 'communities' and performs a two-stage mapping; first at the community level and then for the entire network. Even when nodes cannot be explicitly mapped, the community structure can be mapped between both networks, thus reducing the anonymity of users.

More recently, a two-phase de-anonymisation algorithm is proposed in Ji et al. (2015). They use the digital traces left by users of online social networking services can make the anonymised network susceptible. They have proposed an algorithm, which they call as seed-and-grow to identify users from an anonymised social graph, based solely on graph structure. The advantage of this algorithm is that it identifies and relaxes implicit assumptions taken by previous works, eliminates arbitrary parameters and improves identification effectiveness and accuracy.

Another very recent work on de-anonymisation is due to Su and Shukla (Su et al., 2017) This approach is based upon a simple observation: each person has a distinctive social network and thus the set of links in their feed with higher probability than a random user, browsing histories contain tell-tale marks of identity. This intuition is formalised by them to by specifying a model of web browsing behaviour and then deriving the maximum likelihood estimate of a user's social profile. The contribution applies to any type of transactional data and is robust to noisy observations, generalizing a wide range of previous de-anonymisation attacks.

In Ji et al. (2015), the first comprehensive quantization on the perfect de-anonymisability and partial de-anonymisability of real world, so the effectiveness of anonymisation techniques.\; i. e. researchers can employ this technical networks with seed information in general scenarios, where a social network can follow an arbitrary distribution model. This quantification provides the theoretical foundation for existing structure based de-anonymisation attacks. It closes the gap between de-anonymisation practice and theory. Further this quantification can serve as a testing-stone for the effectiveness of anonymisation techniques; i.e. researchers can employ the quantified structural conditions to evaluate the potential de-anonymisability of the anonymised social networks.

# CONCLUSION

De-anonymisation is the reverse process of anonymisation. Using this technique an anonymised network can be put back into its original form. This is a serious challenge to the researchers working on anonymisation. In this chapter we discussed on various de-anonymisation attacks. We presented an efficient algorithm called the 'Two stage de-anonymisation algorithm'. The proposers of this algorithm claim that this algorithm can de-anonymise any anonymised social network, which has been generated by using any algorithm put forth by researchers till that time. But, that was in 2014. After the publication of this paper several efficient algorithms have been proposed for anonymisation of social networks. So, it will be interesting to see if the situation is like that now also. We also presented some more de-anonymisation algorithms which have been proposed besides the above algorithm.

# REFERENCES

Backstrom, L., Dwork, C., & Kleinberg, J. J. (2007). Wherefore art thou R3579X? Anonymized social networks, hidden patterns, and structural steganography. *Proceedings on the 2007 World Wide Web Conference.* Retrieved from http://www.cs.cornell.edu/~lars/www07-anon.pdf

Carthy, R. (2007). *Will IR SeeK have a chilling effect on IRC chat?* Retrieved from http:// www.techcrunch.com /2007/ 11/ 30/ will-irseek-have-a-chilling-effect-on-irc-chat/

Facebook. (2007). *Facebook's privacy policy.* Retrieved from http://www. new.facebook.com/policy.php

Felt, A., & Evans, D. (2008). Privacy protection for social networking APIs. *Proceedings on Web 2.0 Security & Privacy Conference.*

Frikken, K., & Golle, P. (2006). Private social network analysis: How to assemble pieces of a graph privately. *Proceedings on the Workshop on Privacy in the Electronic Society.* doi:10.1145/1179601.1179619

Guha, S., Tang, K., & Francis, P. (2008). NOYB: Privacy in online social networks. In *Proceedings of the first ACM Workshop on Online Social Networks.* Seattle, WA: ACM. doi:10.1145/1397735.1397747

Hay, M., Miklau, G., Jensen, D., Weis, P., & Srivastava, S. (2007). *Anonymizing social networks. Computer Science Department Faculty Publication Series*. Amherst, MA: University of Massachusetts. Retrieved from http://scholarworks.umass.edu/cs_faculty_pubs/180/

Ji, S., Li, W., Gong, N. Z., Mittal, P., & Beyah, R. (2015) On Your Social Network de-anonymisability: Quantification and Large Scale Evaluation with seed Knowledge. *Proceedings on the Network and Distributed System Security Symposium (NDSS)*.

Lucas, M., & Borisov, N. (2008). flyByNight: Mitigating the privacy risks of social networking. In *Proceedings on the Workshop on Privacy in the Electronic Society*. Alexandria, VA: ACM.

Narayanan, A., & Shmatikov, V. (19 March 2009). De-anonymizing Social Networks. In *Proceedings on 2009 30th IEEE Symposium on Privacy and Security*. Berkley, CA: IEEE. doi:10.1109/SP.2009.22

Nilizadeh, S., Kapadia, A., & Ahn, Y. Y. (2014). Community-Enhanced De-anonymization of Online Social Networks. In *Proceedings of the 2014 Conference on Computer and Communications Security*. Scottsdale, AZ: ACM. doi:10.1145/2660267.2660324

Peng, W., Li, F., Zou, X., & Wu, J. (2014). A Two-stage de-anonymisation attack against anonymised social network. *IEEE Transactions on Computers*, *63*(2), 290–303. doi:10.1109/TC.2012.202

Su, J., Shukla, A., Goel, S., & Narayanan, A. (2017). *De-anonymising Web Browsing Data with Social networks*. ACM.

Zheleva, E., & Getoor, L. (2007). Preserving the privacy of sensitive relationships in graph data. *Proceedings of the 1st ACM SIGKDD international conference on Privacy, security, and trust in KDD*.

Zhou, B., & Pei, J. (2008). Preserving privacy in social networks against neighborhood attacks, In *Proceedings on the 2008 IEEE 24th International Conference on Data Engineering*. Cancun, Mexico: IEEE. doi:10.1109/ICDE.2008.4497459

# Conclusion

## SUMMARY OF THE BOOK AND OUTLOOK

The main objective of this book is to make the readers familiar with social networks, their importance in the modern society, the threats on maintaining their security and the anonymisation techniques proposed so far in the literature as a measure to manage security in social networks.

With this objective in view, we started with a discussion on fundamentals of social networks and the different techniques used to represent social networks. Representation of any concept is required to store them in a computer and use them as inputs to different algorithms in order to operate upon them, analyse their requirements, modify their structure as per requirement and most importantly operate on them. The data structure frequently used to represent a social network is as an adjacency matrix. The graphical representation provides an easy way to view it. Instead of expecting any background knowledge from the users, the concepts related to graphs, matrices and adjacency list are introduced in the beginning. The requirement for anonymisation of social networks lies in the different types of attacks by intruders. So, we presented the types of attacks. Before that we talked about the two important concepts of security and privacy associated with social networks. The development of online social networks is a significant aspect in modern society. We have got more or less addicted to these networks and these networks have become an integral part of our day-to-day lives. So, some of the frequently used and accessed on line social networks are presented to provide the origin of these networks, their functionalities and their current status.

The social networks, if undisclosed would make the volume of information they contain unused for analysis by the researchers. But, disclosure will obviously lead to leakage of secret information of the respondents. This is highly undesirable. So, before publication of these networks or making them open, sufficient precaution must be taken so that both the above are not disturbed; that is the network information will be disclosed but the sensitive information of the respondents will remain intact. Anonymisation of social networks is one such technique. Several factors are involved in anonymisation of social networks. We presented them. The information available with an intruder plays an important role in identifying the respondents and unless it is taken care of an anonymisation technique cannot be successful. As a consequence, most of the anonymisation algorithms take care of this aspect. With this background, we introduced different categories of anonymisation methods. These are broadly grouped into clustering approaches and graph modification approach. While clustering based approaches deal with modification and grouping of vertices and edges, the graph modification approaches deal with overall structure of the associated graphs. In Chapter 2 we discussed on these topics.

In Chapter 3, we focused upon a specific type of attacks, which is termed as neighbourhood attack in the literature, because of its nature in accessing the information about a node from the structure of its neighbourhood. So, we presented a recent algorithm, called GASNA and discussed at length its applicability on real world networks. Clustering approach is perhaps the earliest among all approaches in social network anonymisation. We devoted a full chapter (Chapter 4) on approach and dealt with the important algorithms available on this topic. Also, social networks in use are mostly dynamic by nature. So, we discussed on one efficient algorithm in this direction, namely the "incremental k-clique clustering".

Graph modification algorithms for social network anonymisation are of recent origin. The techniques used in these algorithms include vertex or edge deletion, noise node addition and edge addition. The deletion approaches lead to loss of enough of information and hence are not advisable. Noise node addition is supposed to be a better approach. We have discussed on it. The k-anonymisation techniques are used extensively in the anonymisation of relational databases. Some loopholes have been found in k-anonymity and the concept was extended to propose the concepts of l-diversity and t-closeness in the relational databases. Under l-diversity again, we have three types; distinct l-diversity, entropy base l-diversity and (c, l)- recursive diversity. Recently some algorithms are developed in the context of social networks in this direction. These come under the broad category of $\alpha - anonymisation$. We presented on the most recent algorithms in this direction; namely the $(\alpha, k)anonymity$, $(\alpha, l) - diversity$ and the recursive $(\alpha, c, l) - diversity$ algorithms.

Social networks are directed many a times and also the relations between nodes can also be weighted. So far the social networks considered were undirected and unweighted. So, in Chapter 6 we present the problem of anonymisation for such social networks. Some of the algorithms cover only the weighted case and some others handle the most general case of directed and weighted social networks. Also, a case of transform method used to convert directed social networks into undirected ones is discussed. If a network is only a directed and not a weighted one then it can be transformed to an undirected one, so that the existing algorithms for anonymisation of undirected and unweighted social networks discussed in the earlier chapters can be used to anonymise the networks.

Now, the question comes, whether the anonymised social networks can be de-anonymised to its original for fully or partially. Once an anonymised social network is e-anonymised the intruders can apply their own techniques as for un-anonymised social networks and solve their purpose. It is disheartening to note that some such algorithms exist in literature. These algorithms are also called the re-identification algorithms. The attackers can utilise auxiliary information to achieve this. The auxiliary information can be that the adversary can modify the network before its release by adding a small number if new user accounts with edges to the targeted users (called as active attack) or through passive attacks in which a small coalition of users discovers their location in the anonymised graph by utilising the knowledge of the network structure around them. A two stage de-anonymisation algorithm is presented in chapter 7 in this context. The de-anonymising algorithms are so sure of the efficiency of their algorithms in some case that they have even suggested that the researchers who are developing anonymisation algorithms can use their de-anonymisation algorithms to test the efficiency of their proposed algorithms by applying the de-anonymising algorithms. This is a strong challenge and would neutralize the efforts of so many researchers in developing anonymisation algorithms over the years. However, this claim or suggestion is based upon their observation over a few anonymising algorithms. So, the progress has been there in both the directions of developing social network anonymising algorithms and de-anonymising algorithms.

## FUTURE WORKS

Several problems for further study have been proposed by different authors from time to time. Some of those problems have been solved. Still a large number of problems are unsolved on the privacy of social networks, anonymisation of social networks, de-anonymisation of social networks. We tabulate below some of these problems which have not been solved so far.

1.  In Tripathy (2012) a good number of problems have been stated. We refer to the numbers attached to those problems for reference.
    a.  The problem in Tripathy (2012) (1) has been solved partially, except for the t-closeness part.
    b.  The application of social networks or what is called as utility of the anonymised network has been a problem to handle as the goal of every anonymisation algorithm is to keep the structure of the original network as un-disturbed as possible. However, this problem has not been kept in mind in some of the algorithms developed where edge addition/deletion or noise node addition is carried out for anonymisation.
    c.  A proposal for a rough set based anonymisation of social network was outlined in Tripathy (2012), however, no concrete algorithm was developed.
    d.  As far as l-diversity algorithms for social network anonymisation are considered, the entropy l-diversity is yet to be used.
    e.  The extension of the l-diversity algorithms to the context of t-closeness is yet to be handled.
2.  In Tripathy et al. (2014), a few problems for future studies were presented. So far these problems have not been addressed fully. These are:
    a.  The value of k assigned by user is fixed. This makes the anonymisation cost very high at times. The existing algorithms continuously add nodes to the clusters until the number reaches k and l, which are required for k-anonymity and l-diversity. The maximum number of nodes in a cluster after the clustering phase of the algorithm given in Tripathy et al. (2009) is $k + l - 1$. Suppose for a situation $k = 4$ and $l = 2$. Then the maximum size of a cluster will be 5. Let us consider only 1-neighbourhoods. The degree values in the graph be $d_1, d_2, \ldots d_{max}$. Suppose there are 6 vertices of degree $d_{max}$. Out of these 5 will be added to a cluster. Now one node is left with degree $d_{max}$. In order to make this node 4-anonymous at least 3 nodes of degree $d_{max} - 1$ must be promoted to the degree $d_{max}$. But, if the value of k is flexible then all the 6 nodes of degree $d_{max}$ could have been put into one cluster. So, the problem is to develop algorithm with flexible value of k.

b.   The current algorithms for achieving k-anonymity in social networks consider only structural similarity of nodes. But, in case of online social networks like Face book there are other attributes attached to nodes in addition to this. These attributes are like groups, family relationships, groups etc. These attributes connect multiple users to come together with respect to them. An adversary can use complete or partial knowledge of these attributes to identify a user even in structurally anonymised networks. To solve this problem each node in a group must have k-similar nodes in that group. However, there may be nodes that aren't a member of any group. Hence each of these nodes must also have k-similar nodes in the graph. So, the anonymisation algorithms must be extended to handle these cases.

## REFERENCES

Tripathy, B. K. (2012). Anonymisation of Social networks and Rough Set Approach, Chapter-12. In A. Abraham (Ed.), *Computational Social Networks: Security and Privacy*. London: Springer-Verlag. doi:10.1007/978-1-4471-4051-1_12

Tripathy, B. K., Lakshmi Janaki, K., & Jain, N. (2009). Security against neighbourhood attacks in social networks. *Proceedings of the National Conference on Recent Trends in Soft Computing (NCRTSC'09)*, 216-223.

Tripathy, B. K., Sishodia, M. S., Jain, S., & Mitra, A. (2014). Privacy and Anonymisation in Social Networks. In *Social Networking: Mining, Visualisation and Security*. Springer International Publishing.

# Related Readings

To continue IGI Global's long-standing tradition of advancing innovation through emerging research, please find below a compiled list of recommended IGI Global book chapters and journal articles in the areas of heterogeneous computing, complex network analysis, and high performance computing. These related readings will provide additional information and guidance to further enrich your knowledge and assist you with your own research.

Acharjya, D. P., & Mary, A. G. (2014). Privacy Preservation in Information System. In B. Tripathy & D. Acharjya (Eds.), *Advances in Secure Computing, Internet Services, and Applications* (pp. 49–72). Hershey, PA: IGI Global. doi:10.4018/978-1-4666-4940-8.ch003

Adhikari, M., Das, A., & Mukherjee, A. (2016). Utility Computing and Its Utilization. In G. Deka, G. Siddesh, K. Srinivasa, & L. Patnaik (Eds.), *Emerging Research Surrounding Power Consumption and Performance Issues in Utility Computing* (pp. 1–21). Hershey, PA: IGI Global. doi:10.4018/978-1-4666-8853-7.ch001

Adhikari, M., & Kar, S. (2016). Advanced Topics GPU Programming and CUDA Architecture. In G. Deka, G. Siddesh, K. Srinivasa, & L. Patnaik (Eds.), *Emerging Research Surrounding Power Consumption and Performance Issues in Utility Computing* (pp. 175–203). Hershey, PA: IGI Global. doi:10.4018/978-1-4666-8853-7.ch008

Adhikari, M., & Roy, D. (2016). Green Computing. In G. Deka, G. Siddesh, K. Srinivasa, & L. Patnaik (Eds.), *Emerging Research Surrounding Power Consumption and Performance Issues in Utility Computing* (pp. 84–108). Hershey, PA: IGI Global. doi:10.4018/978-1-4666-8853-7.ch005

Ahmad, K., Kumar, G., Wahid, A., & Kirmani, M. M. (2016). Software Performance Estimate using Fuzzy Based Backpropagation Learning. In G. Deka, G. Siddesh, K. Srinivasa, & L. Patnaik (Eds.), *Emerging Research Surrounding Power Consumption and Performance Issues in Utility Computing* (pp. 320–344). Hershey, PA: IGI Global. doi:10.4018/978-1-4666-8853-7.ch016

Ahmed, M. S., Houser, J., Hoque, M. A., Raju, R., & Pfeiffer, P. (2017). Reducing Inter-Process Communication Overhead in Parallel Sparse Matrix-Matrix Multiplication. *International Journal of Grid and High Performance Computing*, 9(3), 46–59. doi:10.4018/IJGHPC.2017070104

Akram, V. K., & Dagdeviren, O. (2016). On k-Connectivity Problems in Distributed Systems. In N. Meghanathan (Ed.), *Advanced Methods for Complex Network Analysis* (pp. 30–57). Hershey, PA: IGI Global. doi:10.4018/978-1-4666-9964-9.ch002

Alfredson, J., & Ohlander, U. (2015). Intelligent Fighter Pilot Support for Distributed Unmanned and Manned Decision Making. In K. Sarma, M. Sarma, & M. Sarma (Eds.), *Intelligent Applications for Heterogeneous System Modeling and Design* (pp. 1–22). Hershey, PA: IGI Global. doi:10.4018/978-1-4666-8493-5.ch001

Alling, A., Powers, N. R., & Soyata, T. (2016). Face Recognition: A Tutorial on Computational Aspects. In G. Deka, G. Siddesh, K. Srinivasa, & L. Patnaik (Eds.), *Emerging Research Surrounding Power Consumption and Performance Issues in Utility Computing* (pp. 405–425). Hershey, PA: IGI Global. doi:10.4018/978-1-4666-8853-7.ch020

Alsarhan, A., Abdallah, E. E., & Aljammal, A. H. (2017). Competitive Processors Allocation in 2D Mesh Connected Multicomputer Networks: A Dynamic Game Approach. *International Journal of Grid and High Performance Computing*, 9(2), 53–69. doi:10.4018/IJGHPC.2017040104

Amitab, K., Kandar, D., & Maji, A. K. (2016). Speckle Noise Filtering Using Back-Propagation Multi-Layer Perceptron Network in Synthetic Aperture Radar Image. In P. Mallick (Ed.), *Research Advances in the Integration of Big Data and Smart Computing* (pp. 280–301). Hershey, PA: IGI Global. doi:10.4018/978-1-4666-8737-0.ch016

Aslanpour, M. S., & Dashti, S. E. (2017). Proactive Auto-Scaling Algorithm (PASA) for Cloud Application. *International Journal of Grid and High Performance Computing*, *9*(3), 1–16. doi:10.4018/IJGHPC.2017070101

Balluff, S., Bendfeld, J., & Krauter, S. (2017). Meteorological Data Forecast using RNN. *International Journal of Grid and High Performance Computing*, *9*(1), 61–74. doi:10.4018/IJGHPC.2017010106

Baragi, S., & Iyer, N. C. (2016). Face Recognition using Fast Fourier Transform. In P. Mallick (Ed.), *Research Advances in the Integration of Big Data and Smart Computing* (pp. 302–322). Hershey, PA: IGI Global. doi:10.4018/978-1-4666-8737-0.ch017

Benson, I., Kaplan, A., Flynn, J., & Katz, S. (2017). Fault-Tolerant and Deterministic Flight-Software System For a High Performance CubeSat. *International Journal of Grid and High Performance Computing*, *9*(1), 92–104. doi:10.4018/IJGHPC.2017010108

Bhadoria, R. S. (2016). Performance of Enterprise Architecture in Utility Computing. In G. Deka, G. Siddesh, K. Srinivasa, & L. Patnaik (Eds.), *Emerging Research Surrounding Power Consumption and Performance Issues in Utility Computing* (pp. 44–68). Hershey, PA: IGI Global. doi:10.4018/978-1-4666-8853-7.ch003

Bhadoria, R. S., & Patil, C. (2016). Adaptive Mobile Architecture with Utility Computing. In G. Deka, G. Siddesh, K. Srinivasa, & L. Patnaik (Eds.), *Emerging Research Surrounding Power Consumption and Performance Issues in Utility Computing* (pp. 386–404). Hershey, PA: IGI Global. doi:10.4018/978-1-4666-8853-7.ch019

Bhargavi, K., & Babu, B. S. (2016). GPU Computation and Platforms. In G. Deka, G. Siddesh, K. Srinivasa, & L. Patnaik (Eds.), *Emerging Research Surrounding Power Consumption and Performance Issues in Utility Computing* (pp. 136–174). Hershey, PA: IGI Global. doi:10.4018/978-1-4666-8853-7.ch007

Bhat, C. G., & Kopparapu, S. K. (2017). Creating Sound Glyph Database for Video Subtitling. In M. S., & V. V. (Eds.), Multi-Core Computer Vision and Image Processing for Intelligent Applications (pp. 136-154). Hershey, PA: IGI Global. doi:10.4018/978-1-5225-0889-2.ch005

Bhoi, A. K., Sherpa, K. S., & Khandelwal, B. (2016). Baseline Drift Removal of ECG Signal: Comparative Analysis of Filtering Techniques. In P. Mallick (Ed.), *Research Advances in the Integration of Big Data and Smart Computing* (pp. 134–152). Hershey, PA: IGI Global. doi:10.4018/978-1-4666-8737-0. ch008

Bhura, M., Deshpande, P. H., & Chandrasekaran, K. (2016). CUDA or OpenCL: Which is Better? A Detailed Performance Analysis. In P. Mallick (Ed.), *Research Advances in the Integration of Big Data and Smart Computing* (pp. 267–279). Hershey, PA: IGI Global. doi:10.4018/978-1-4666-8737-0.ch015

Bisoy, S. K., & Pattnaik, P. K. (2016). Transmission Control Protocol for Mobile Ad Hoc Network. In P. Mallick (Ed.), *Research Advances in the Integration of Big Data and Smart Computing* (pp. 22–49). Hershey, PA: IGI Global. doi:10.4018/978-1-4666-8737-0.ch002

Borovikov, E., Vajda, S., Lingappa, G., & Bonifant, M. C. (2017). Parallel Computing in Face Image Retrieval: Practical Approach to the Real-World Image Search. In M. S., & V. V. (Eds.), Multi-Core Computer Vision and Image Processing for Intelligent Applications (pp. 155-189). Hershey, PA: IGI Global. doi:10.4018/978-1-5225-0889-2.ch006

Casillas, L., Daradoumis, T., & Caballe, S. (2016). A Network Analysis Method for Tailoring Academic Programs. In N. Meghanathan (Ed.), *Advanced Methods for Complex Network Analysis* (pp. 396–417). Hershey, PA: IGI Global. doi:10.4018/978-1-4666-9964-9.ch017

Chauhan, R., & Kaur, H. (2014). Predictive Analytics and Data Mining: A Framework for Optimizing Decisions with R Tool. In B. Tripathy & D. Acharjya (Eds.), *Advances in Secure Computing, Internet Services, and Applications* (pp. 73–88). Hershey, PA: IGI Global. doi:10.4018/978-1-4666-4940-8.ch004

Chen, G., Wang, E., Sun, X., & Lu, Y. (2016). An Intelligent Approval System for City Construction based on Cloud Computing and Big Data. *International Journal of Grid and High Performance Computing, 8*(3), 57–69. doi:10.4018/ IJGHPC.2016070104

Chen, Z., Yang, S., Shang, Y., Liu, Y., Wang, F., Wang, L., & Fu, J. (2016). Fragment Re-Allocation Strategy Based on Hypergraph for NoSQL Database Systems. *International Journal of Grid and High Performance Computing, 8*(3), 1–23. doi:10.4018/IJGHPC.2016070101

Choudhury, A., Talukdar, A. K., & Sarma, K. K. (2015). A Review on Vision-Based Hand Gesture Recognition and Applications. In K. Sarma, M. Sarma, & M. Sarma (Eds.), *Intelligent Applications for Heterogeneous System Modeling and Design* (pp. 256–281). Hershey, PA: IGI Global. doi:10.4018/978-1-4666-8493-5.ch011

Coti, C. (2016). Fault Tolerance Techniques for Distributed, Parallel Applications. In Q. Hassan (Ed.), *Innovative Research and Applications in Next-Generation High Performance Computing* (pp. 221–252). Hershey, PA: IGI Global. doi:10.4018/978-1-5225-0287-6.ch009

Crespo, M. L., Cicuttin, A., Gazzano, J. D., & Rincon Calle, F. (2016). Reconfigurable Virtual Instrumentation Based on FPGA for Science and High-Education. In J. Gazzano, M. Crespo, A. Cicuttin, & F. Calle (Eds.), *Field-Programmable Gate Array (FPGA) Technologies for High Performance Instrumentation* (pp. 99–123). Hershey, PA: IGI Global. doi:10.4018/978-1-5225-0299-9.ch005

Daniel, D. K., & Bhandari, V. (2014). Neural Network Model to Estimate and Predict Cell Mass Concentration in Lipase Fermentation. In B. Tripathy & D. Acharjya (Eds.), *Advances in Secure Computing, Internet Services, and Applications* (pp. 303–316). Hershey, PA: IGI Global. doi:10.4018/978-1-4666-4940-8.ch015

Das, B., Sarma, M. P., & Sarma, K. K. (2015). Different Aspects of Interleaving Techniques in Wireless Communication. In K. Sarma, M. Sarma, & M. Sarma (Eds.), *Intelligent Applications for Heterogeneous System Modeling and Design* (pp. 335–374). Hershey, PA: IGI Global. doi:10.4018/978-1-4666-8493-5.ch015

Das, P. K. (2016). Comparative Study on XEN, KVM, VSphere, and Hyper-V. In G. Deka, G. Siddesh, K. Srinivasa, & L. Patnaik (Eds.), *Emerging Research Surrounding Power Consumption and Performance Issues in Utility Computing* (pp. 233–261). Hershey, PA: IGI Global. doi:10.4018/978-1-4666-8853-7.ch011

Das, P. K., & Deka, G. C. (2016). History and Evolution of GPU Architecture. In G. Deka, G. Siddesh, K. Srinivasa, & L. Patnaik (Eds.), *Emerging Research Surrounding Power Consumption and Performance Issues in Utility Computing* (pp. 109–135). Hershey, PA: IGI Global. doi:10.4018/978-1-4666-8853-7.ch006

Das, R., & Pradhan, M. K. (2014). Artificial Neural Network Modeling for Electrical Discharge Machining Parameters. In B. Tripathy & D. Acharjya (Eds.), *Advances in Secure Computing, Internet Services, and Applications* (pp. 281–302). Hershey, PA: IGI Global. doi:10.4018/978-1-4666-4940-8.ch014

Das, S., & Kalita, H. K. (2016). Advanced Dimensionality Reduction Method for Big Data. In P. Mallick (Ed.), *Research Advances in the Integration of Big Data and Smart Computing* (pp. 198–210). Hershey, PA: IGI Global. doi:10.4018/978-1-4666-8737-0.ch011

Das, S., & Kalita, H. K. (2016). Efficient Classification Rule Mining for Breast Cancer Detection. In P. Mallick (Ed.), *Research Advances in the Integration of Big Data and Smart Computing* (pp. 50–63). Hershey, PA: IGI Global. doi:10.4018/978-1-4666-8737-0.ch003

De Micco, L., & Larrondo, H. A. (2016). Methodology for FPGA Implementation of a Chaos-Based AWGN Generator. In J. Gazzano, M. Crespo, A. Cicuttin, & F. Calle (Eds.), *Field-Programmable Gate Array (FPGA) Technologies for High Performance Instrumentation* (pp. 43–58). Hershey, PA: IGI Global. doi:10.4018/978-1-5225-0299-9.ch003

de Souza, E. D., & Lima, E. J. II. (2017). Autonomic Computing in a Biomimetic Algorithm for Robots Dedicated to Rehabilitation of Ankle. *International Journal of Grid and High Performance Computing, 9*(1), 48–60. doi:10.4018/IJGHPC.2017010105

Deepika, R., Prasad, M. R., Chetana, S., & Manjunath, T. C. (2016). Adoption of Dual Iris and Periocular Recognition for Human Identification. In P. Mallick (Ed.), *Research Advances in the Integration of Big Data and Smart Computing* (pp. 250–266). Hershey, PA: IGI Global. doi:10.4018/978-1-4666-8737-0.ch014

Dey, P., & Roy, S. (2016). Social Network Analysis. In N. Meghanathan (Ed.), *Advanced Methods for Complex Network Analysis* (pp. 237–265). Hershey, PA: IGI Global. doi:10.4018/978-1-4666-9964-9.ch010

Don Clark, A. (2016). A Theoretic Representation of the Effects of Targeted Failures in HPC Systems. In Q. Hassan (Ed.), *Innovative Research and Applications in Next-Generation High Performance Computing* (pp. 253–276). Hershey, PA: IGI Global. doi:10.4018/978-1-5225-0287-6.ch010

Dutta, P., & Ojha, V. K. (2014). Conjugate Gradient Trained Neural Network for Intelligent Sensing of Manhole Gases to Avoid Human Fatality. In B. Tripathy & D. Acharjya (Eds.), *Advances in Secure Computing, Internet Services, and Applications* (pp. 257–280). Hershey, PA: IGI Global. doi:10.4018/978-1-4666-4940-8.ch013

Elkhodr, M., Shahrestani, S., & Cheung, H. (2016). Internet of Things Applications: Current and Future Development. In Q. Hassan (Ed.), *Innovative Research and Applications in Next-Generation High Performance Computing* (pp. 397–427). Hershey, PA: IGI Global. doi:10.4018/978-1-5225-0287-6. ch016

Elkhodr, M., Shahrestani, S., & Cheung, H. (2016). Wireless Enabling Technologies for the Internet of Things. In Q. Hassan (Ed.), *Innovative Research and Applications in Next-Generation High Performance Computing* (pp. 368–396). Hershey, PA: IGI Global. doi:10.4018/978-1-5225-0287-6.ch015

Elmisery, A. M., & Sertovic, M. (2017). Privacy Enhanced Cloud-Based Recommendation Service for Implicit Discovery of Relevant Support Groups in Healthcare Social Networks. *International Journal of Grid and High Performance Computing, 9*(1), 75–91. doi:10.4018/IJGHPC.2017010107

Fazio, P., Tropea, M., Marano, S., & Curia, V. (2016). A Hybrid Complex Network Model for Wireless Sensor Networks and Performance Evaluation. In N. Meghanathan (Ed.), *Advanced Methods for Complex Network Analysis* (pp. 379–395). Hershey, PA: IGI Global. doi:10.4018/978-1-4666-9964-9.ch016

Fei, X., Li, K., Yang, W., & Li, K. (2016). CPU-GPU Computing: Overview, Optimization, and Applications. In Q. Hassan (Ed.), *Innovative Research and Applications in Next-Generation High Performance Computing* (pp. 159–193). Hershey, PA: IGI Global. doi:10.4018/978-1-5225-0287-6.ch007

Funes, M. A., Hadad, M. N., Donato, P. G., & Carrica, D. O. (2016). Optimization of Advanced Signal Processing Architectures for Detection of Signals Immersed in Noise. In J. Gazzano, M. Crespo, A. Cicuttin, & F. Calle (Eds.), *Field-Programmable Gate Array (FPGA) Technologies for High Performance Instrumentation* (pp. 171–212). Hershey, PA: IGI Global. doi:10.4018/978-1-5225-0299-9.ch008

Garcia-Robledo, A., Diaz-Perez, A., & Morales-Luna, G. (2016). Characterization and Coarsening of Autonomous System Networks: Measuring and Simplifying the Internet. In N. Meghanathan (Ed.), *Advanced Methods for Complex Network Analysis* (pp. 148–179). Hershey, PA: IGI Global. doi:10.4018/978-1-4666-9964-9.ch006

Garg, A., Biswas, A., & Biswas, B. (2016). Evolutionary Computation Techniques for Community Detection in Social Network Analysis. In N. Meghanathan (Ed.), *Advanced Methods for Complex Network Analysis* (pp. 266–284). Hershey, PA: IGI Global. doi:10.4018/978-1-4666-9964-9.ch011

Garg, P., & Gupta, A. (2016). Restoration Technique to Optimize Recovery Time for Efficient OSPF Network. In P. Mallick (Ed.), *Research Advances in the Integration of Big Data and Smart Computing* (pp. 64–88). Hershey, PA: IGI Global. doi:10.4018/978-1-4666-8737-0.ch004

Gazzano, J. D., Calle, F. R., Caba, J., de la Fuente, D., & Romero, J. B. (2016). Dynamic Reconfiguration for Internal Monitoring Services. In J. Gazzano, M. Crespo, A. Cicuttin, & F. Calle (Eds.), *Field-Programmable Gate Array (FPGA) Technologies for High Performance Instrumentation* (pp. 124–136). Hershey, PA: IGI Global. doi:10.4018/978-1-5225-0299-9.ch006

Geethanjali, P. (2014). Pattern Recognition and Robotics. In B. Tripathy & D. Acharjya (Eds.), *Advances in Secure Computing, Internet Services, and Applications* (pp. 35–48). Hershey, PA: IGI Global. doi:10.4018/978-1-4666-4940-8.ch002

Ghai, D., & Jain, N. (2016). Signal Processing: Iteration Bound and Loop Bound. In P. Mallick (Ed.), *Research Advances in the Integration of Big Data and Smart Computing* (pp. 153–177). Hershey, PA: IGI Global. doi:10.4018/978-1-4666-8737-0.ch009

Ghaiwat, S. N., & Arora, P. (2016). Cotton Leaf Disease Detection by Feature Extraction. In P. Mallick (Ed.), *Research Advances in the Integration of Big Data and Smart Computing* (pp. 89–104). Hershey, PA: IGI Global. doi:10.4018/978-1-4666-8737-0.ch005

Ghorpade-Aher, J., Pagare, R., Thengade, A., Ghorpade, S., & Kadam, M. (2016). Big Data: The Data Deluge. In P. Mallick (Ed.), *Research Advances in the Integration of Big Data and Smart Computing* (pp. 1–21). Hershey, PA: IGI Global. doi:10.4018/978-1-4666-8737-0.ch001

Gil-Costa, V., Molina, R. S., Petrino, R., Paez, C. F., Printista, A. M., & Gazzano, J. D. (2016). Hardware Acceleration of CBIR System with FPGA-Based Platform. In J. Gazzano, M. Crespo, A. Cicuttin, & F. Calle (Eds.), *Field-Programmable Gate Array (FPGA) Technologies for High Performance Instrumentation* (pp. 138–170). Hershey, PA: IGI Global. doi:10.4018/978-1-5225-0299-9.ch007

Goswami, S., Mehjabin, S., & Kashyap, P. A. (2015). Driverless Metro Train with Automatic Crowd Control System. In K. Sarma, M. Sarma, & M. Sarma (Eds.), *Intelligent Applications for Heterogeneous System Modeling and Design* (pp. 76–95). Hershey, PA: IGI Global. doi:10.4018/978-1-4666-8493-5.ch004

Guan, Q., DeBardeleben, N., Blanchard, S., Fu, S., Davis, C. H. IV, & Jones, W. M. (2016). Analyzing the Robustness of HPC Applications Using a Fine-Grained Soft Error Fault Injection Tool. In Q. Hassan (Ed.), *Innovative Research and Applications in Next-Generation High Performance Computing* (pp. 277–305). Hershey, PA: IGI Global. doi:10.4018/978-1-5225-0287-6.ch011

Guerrero, J. I., Monedero, Í., Biscarri, F., Biscarri, J., Millán, R., & León, C. (2014). Detection of Non-Technical Losses: The Project MIDAS. In B. Tripathy & D. Acharjya (Eds.), *Advances in Secure Computing, Internet Services, and Applications* (pp. 140–164). Hershey, PA: IGI Global. doi:10.4018/978-1-4666-4940-8.ch008

Habbal, A., Abdullah, S. A., Mkpojiogu, E. O., Hassan, S., & Benamar, N. (2017). Assessing Experimental Private Cloud Using Web of System Performance Model. *International Journal of Grid and High Performance Computing*, 9(2), 21–35. doi:10.4018/IJGHPC.2017040102

Habib, I., Islam, A., Chetia, S., & Saikia, S. J. (2015). A New Coding Scheme for Data Security in RF based Wireless Communication. In K. Sarma, M. Sarma, & M. Sarma (Eds.), *Intelligent Applications for Heterogeneous System Modeling and Design* (pp. 301–319). Hershey, PA: IGI Global. doi:10.4018/978-1-4666-8493-5.ch013

Hamilton, H., & Alasti, H. (2017). Controlled Intelligent Agents' Security Model for Multi-Tenant Cloud Computing Infrastructures. *International Journal of Grid and High Performance Computing*, 9(1), 1–13. doi:10.4018/IJGHPC.2017010101

Ileri, C. U., Ural, C. A., Dagdeviren, O., & Kavalci, V. (2016). On Vertex Cover Problems in Distributed Systems. In N. Meghanathan (Ed.), *Advanced Methods for Complex Network Analysis* (pp. 1–29). Hershey, PA: IGI Global. doi:10.4018/978-1-4666-9964-9.ch001

Ingale, A. G. (2014). Prediction of Structural and Functional Aspects of Protein: In-Silico Approach. In B. Tripathy & D. Acharjya (Eds.), *Advances in Secure Computing, Internet Services, and Applications* (pp. 317–333). Hershey, PA: IGI Global. doi:10.4018/978-1-4666-4940-8.ch016

Jadon, K. S., Mudgal, P., & Bhadoria, R. S. (2016). Optimization and Management of Resource in Utility Computing. In G. Deka, G. Siddesh, K. Srinivasa, & L. Patnaik (Eds.), *Emerging Research Surrounding Power Consumption and Performance Issues in Utility Computing* (pp. 22–43). Hershey, PA: IGI Global. doi:10.4018/978-1-4666-8853-7.ch002

K. G. S., G. M., S., Hiriyannaiah, S., Morappanavar, A., & Banerjee, A. (2016). A Novel Approach of Symmetric Key Cryptography using Genetic Algorithm Implemented on GPGPU. In G. Deka, G. Siddesh, K. Srinivasa, & L. Patnaik (Eds.), Emerging Research Surrounding Power Consumption and Performance Issues in Utility Computing (pp. 283-303). Hershey, PA: IGI Global. doi:10.4018/978-1-4666-8853-7.ch014

Kannan, R. (2014). Graphical Evaluation and Review Technique (GERT): The Panorama in the Computation and Visualization of Network-Based Project Management. In B. Tripathy & D. Acharjya (Eds.), *Advances in Secure Computing, Internet Services, and Applications* (pp. 165–179). Hershey, PA: IGI Global. doi:10.4018/978-1-4666-4940-8.ch009

Kasemsap, K. (2014). The Role of Knowledge Management on Job Satisfaction: A Systematic Framework. In B. Tripathy & D. Acharjya (Eds.), *Advances in Secure Computing, Internet Services, and Applications* (pp. 104–127). Hershey, PA: IGI Global. doi:10.4018/978-1-4666-4940-8.ch006

Khadtare, M. S. (2016). GPU Based Image Quality Assessment using Structural Similarity (SSIM) Index. In G. Deka, G. Siddesh, K. Srinivasa, & L. Patnaik (Eds.), *Emerging Research Surrounding Power Consumption and Performance Issues in Utility Computing* (pp. 276–282). Hershey, PA: IGI Global. doi:10.4018/978-1-4666-8853-7.ch013

Khan, A. U., & Khan, A. N. (2016). High Performance Computing on Mobile Devices. In Q. Hassan (Ed.), *Innovative Research and Applications in Next-Generation High Performance Computing* (pp. 334–348). Hershey, PA: IGI Global. doi:10.4018/978-1-5225-0287-6.ch013

Khan, M. S. (2016). A Study of Computer Virus Propagation on Scale Free Networks Using Differential Equations. In N. Meghanathan (Ed.), *Advanced Methods for Complex Network Analysis* (pp. 196–214). Hershey, PA: IGI Global. doi:10.4018/978-1-4666-9964-9.ch008

Khan, R. H. (2015). Utilizing UML, cTLA, and SRN: An Application to Distributed System Performance Modeling. In K. Sarma, M. Sarma, & M. Sarma (Eds.), *Intelligent Applications for Heterogeneous System Modeling and Design* (pp. 23–50). Hershey, PA: IGI Global. doi:10.4018/978-1-4666-8493-5.ch002

Konwar, P., & Bordoloi, H. (2015). An EOG Signal based Framework to Control a Wheel Chair. In K. Sarma, M. Sarma, & M. Sarma (Eds.), *Intelligent Applications for Heterogeneous System Modeling and Design* (pp. 51–75). Hershey, PA: IGI Global. doi:10.4018/978-1-4666-8493-5.ch003

Koppad, S. H., & Shwetha, T. M. (2016). Indic Language: Kannada to Braille Conversion Tool Using Client Server Architecture Model. In P. Mallick (Ed.), *Research Advances in the Integration of Big Data and Smart Computing* (pp. 120–133). Hershey, PA: IGI Global. doi:10.4018/978-1-4666-8737-0.ch007

Kumar, P. S., Pradhan, S. K., & Panda, S. (2016). The Pedagogy of English Teaching-Learning at Primary Level in Rural Government Schools: A Data Mining View. In P. Mallick (Ed.), *Research Advances in the Integration of Big Data and Smart Computing* (pp. 105–119). Hershey, PA: IGI Global. doi:10.4018/978-1-4666-8737-0.ch006

Kumar, S., Ranjan, P., Ramaswami, R., & Tripathy, M. R. (2017). Resource Efficient Clustering and Next Hop Knowledge Based Routing in Multiple Heterogeneous Wireless Sensor Networks. *International Journal of Grid and High Performance Computing*, 9(2), 1–20. doi:10.4018/IJGHPC.2017040101

Kunfang, S., & Lu, H. (2016). Efficient Querying Distributed Big-XML Data using MapReduce. *International Journal of Grid and High Performance Computing*, 8(3), 70–79. doi:10.4018/IJGHPC.2016070105

Li, Y., Zhai, J., & Li, K. (2016). Communication Analysis and Performance Prediction of Parallel Applications on Large-Scale Machines. In Q. Hassan (Ed.), *Innovative Research and Applications in Next-Generation High Performance Computing* (pp. 80–105). Hershey, PA: IGI Global. doi:10.4018/978-1-5225-0287-6.ch005

Lin, L., Li, S., Li, B., Zhan, J., & Zhao, Y. (2016). TVGuarder: A Trace-Enable Virtualization Protection Framework against Insider Threats for IaaS Environments. *International Journal of Grid and High Performance Computing, 8*(4), 1–20. doi:10.4018/IJGHPC.2016100101

López, M. B. (2017). Mobile Platform Challenges in Interactive Computer Vision. In M. S., & V. V. (Eds.), Multi-Core Computer Vision and Image Processing for Intelligent Applications (pp. 47-73). Hershey, PA: IGI Global. doi:10.4018/978-1-5225-0889-2.ch002

Maarouf, A., El Qacimy, B., Marzouk, A., & Haqiq, A. (2017). Defining and Evaluating A Novel Penalty Model for Managing Violations in the Cloud Computing. *International Journal of Grid and High Performance Computing, 9*(2), 36–52. doi:10.4018/IJGHPC.2017040103

Mahmoud, I. I. (2016). Implementation of Reactor Control Rod Position Sensing/Display Using a VLSI Chip. In J. Gazzano, M. Crespo, A. Cicuttin, & F. Calle (Eds.), *Field-Programmable Gate Array (FPGA) Technologies for High Performance Instrumentation* (pp. 1–16). Hershey, PA: IGI Global. doi:10.4018/978-1-5225-0299-9.ch001

Mahmoud, I. I., & El Tokhy, M. S. (2016). Development of Algorithms and Their Hardware Implementation for Gamma Radiation Spectrometry. In J. Gazzano, M. Crespo, A. Cicuttin, & F. Calle (Eds.), *Field-Programmable Gate Array (FPGA) Technologies for High Performance Instrumentation* (pp. 17–41). Hershey, PA: IGI Global. doi:10.4018/978-1-5225-0299-9.ch002

Mahmoud, I. I., Salama, M., & El Hamid, A. A. (2016). Hardware Implementation of a Genetic Algorithm for Motion Path Planning. In J. Gazzano, M. Crespo, A. Cicuttin, & F. Calle (Eds.), *Field-Programmable Gate Array (FPGA) Technologies for High Performance Instrumentation* (pp. 250–275). Hershey, PA: IGI Global. doi:10.4018/978-1-5225-0299-9.ch010

Maji, A. K., Rymbai, B., & Kandar, D. (2016). A Study on Different Facial Features Extraction Technique. In P. Mallick (Ed.), *Research Advances in the Integration of Big Data and Smart Computing* (pp. 224–249). Hershey, PA: IGI Global. doi:10.4018/978-1-4666-8737-0.ch013

Mallick, P. K., Mohanty, M. N., & Kumar, S. S. (2016). White Patch Detection in Brain MRI Image Using Evolutionary Clustering Algorithm. In P. Mallick (Ed.), *Research Advances in the Integration of Big Data and Smart Computing* (pp. 323–339). Hershey, PA: IGI Global. doi:10.4018/978-1-4666-8737-0.ch018

Mandal, B., Sarma, M. P., & Sarma, K. K. (2015). Design of a Power Aware Systolic Array based Support Vector Machine Classifier. In K. Sarma, M. Sarma, & M. Sarma (Eds.), *Intelligent Applications for Heterogeneous System Modeling and Design* (pp. 96–138). Hershey, PA: IGI Global. doi:10.4018/978-1-4666-8493-5.ch005

Manjaiah, D. H., & Payaswini, P. (2014). Design Issues of 4G-Network Mobility Management. In B. Tripathy & D. Acharjya (Eds.), *Advances in Secure Computing, Internet Services, and Applications* (pp. 210–238). Hershey, PA: IGI Global. doi:10.4018/978-1-4666-4940-8.ch011

Martinez-Gonzalez, R. F., Vazquez-Medina, R., Diaz-Mendez, J. A., & Lopez-Hernandez, J. (2016). FPGA Implementations for Chaotic Maps Using Fixed-Point and Floating-Point Representations. In J. Gazzano, M. Crespo, A. Cicuttin, & F. Calle (Eds.), *Field-Programmable Gate Array (FPGA) Technologies for High Performance Instrumentation* (pp. 59–97). Hershey, PA: IGI Global. doi:10.4018/978-1-5225-0299-9.ch004

Meddah, I. H., & Belkadi, K. (2017). Parallel Distributed Patterns Mining Using Hadoop MapReduce Framework. *International Journal of Grid and High Performance Computing*, 9(2), 70–85. doi:10.4018/IJGHPC.2017040105

Medhi, J. P. (2015). An Approach for Automatic Detection and Grading of Macular Edema. In K. Sarma, M. Sarma, & M. Sarma (Eds.), *Intelligent Applications for Heterogeneous System Modeling and Design* (pp. 204–231). Hershey, PA: IGI Global. doi:10.4018/978-1-4666-8493-5.ch009

Mishra, B. K., & Sahoo, A. K. (2016). Application of Big Data in Economic Policy. In P. Mallick (Ed.), *Research Advances in the Integration of Big Data and Smart Computing* (pp. 178–197). Hershey, PA: IGI Global. doi:10.4018/978-1-4666-8737-0.ch010

Mohan Khilar, P. (2014). Genetic Algorithms: Application to Fault Diagnosis in Distributed Embedded Systems. In B. Tripathy & D. Acharjya (Eds.), *Advances in Secure Computing, Internet Services, and Applications* (pp. 239–255). Hershey, PA: IGI Global. doi:10.4018/978-1-4666-4940-8.ch012

Mohanty, R. P., Turuk, A. K., & Sahoo, B. (2016). Designing of High Performance Multicore Processor with Improved Cache Configuration and Interconnect. In G. Deka, G. Siddesh, K. Srinivasa, & L. Patnaik (Eds.), *Emerging Research Surrounding Power Consumption and Performance Issues in Utility Computing* (pp. 204–219). Hershey, PA: IGI Global. doi:10.4018/978-1-4666-8853-7.ch009

Mohanty, S., Patra, P. K., & Mohapatra, S. (2016). Dynamic Task Assignment with Load Balancing in Cloud Platform. In G. Deka, G. Siddesh, K. Srinivasa, & L. Patnaik (Eds.), *Emerging Research Surrounding Power Consumption and Performance Issues in Utility Computing* (pp. 363–385). Hershey, PA: IGI Global. doi:10.4018/978-1-4666-8853-7.ch018

Mukherjee, A., Chatterjee, A., Das, D., & Naskar, M. K. (2016). Design of Structural Controllability for Complex Network Architecture. In N. Meghanathan (Ed.), *Advanced Methods for Complex Network Analysis* (pp. 98–124). Hershey, PA: IGI Global. doi:10.4018/978-1-4666-9964-9.ch004

Mukherjee, M. Kamarujjaman, & Maitra, M. (2016). Application of Biomedical Image Processing in Blood Cell Counting using Hough Transform. In N. Meghanathan (Ed.), Advanced Methods for Complex Network Analysis (pp. 359-378). Hershey, PA: IGI Global. doi:10.4018/978-1-4666-9964-9.ch015

Naseera, S. (2016). Dynamic Job Scheduling Strategy for Unreliable Nodes in a Volunteer Desktop Grid. *International Journal of Grid and High Performance Computing*, 8(4), 21–33. doi:10.4018/IJGHPC.2016100102

Netake, A., & Katti, P. K. (2016). HTLS Conductors: A Novel Aspect for Energy Conservation in Transmission System. In P. Mallick (Ed.), *Research Advances in the Integration of Big Data and Smart Computing* (pp. 211–223). Hershey, PA: IGI Global. doi:10.4018/978-1-4666-8737-0.ch012

Nirmala, S. R., & Sarma, P. (2015). A Computer Based System for ECG Arrhythmia Classification. In K. Sarma, M. Sarma, & M. Sarma (Eds.), *Intelligent Applications for Heterogeneous System Modeling and Design* (pp. 160–185). Hershey, PA: IGI Global. doi:10.4018/978-1-4666-8493-5.ch007

Nirmala, S. R., & Sharma, P. (2015). Computer Assisted Methods for Retinal Image Classification. In K. Sarma, M. Sarma, & M. Sarma (Eds.), *Intelligent Applications for Heterogeneous System Modeling and Design* (pp. 232–255). Hershey, PA: IGI Global. doi:10.4018/978-1-4666-8493-5.ch010

Omar, M., Ahmad, K., & Rizvi, M. (2016). Content Based Image Retrieval System. In G. Deka, G. Siddesh, K. Srinivasa, & L. Patnaik (Eds.), *Emerging Research Surrounding Power Consumption and Performance Issues in Utility Computing* (pp. 345–362). Hershey, PA: IGI Global. doi:10.4018/978-1-4666-8853-7.ch017

Panda, M., & Patra, M. R. (2014). Characterizing Intelligent Intrusion Detection and Prevention Systems Using Data Mining. In B. Tripathy & D. Acharjya (Eds.), *Advances in Secure Computing, Internet Services, and Applications* (pp. 89–102). Hershey, PA: IGI Global. doi:10.4018/978-1-4666-4940-8.ch005

Pang, X., Wan, B., Li, H., & Lin, W. (2016). MR-LDA: An Efficient Topic Model for Classification of Short Text in Big Social Data. *International Journal of Grid and High Performance Computing, 8*(4), 100–113. doi:10.4018/IJGHPC.2016100106

Perera, D. R., Mannathunga, K. S., Dharmasiri, R. A., Meegama, R. G., & Jayananda, K. (2016). Implementation of a Smart Sensor Node for Wireless Sensor Network Applications Using FPGAs. In J. Gazzano, M. Crespo, A. Cicuttin, & F. Calle (Eds.), *Field-Programmable Gate Array (FPGA) Technologies for High Performance Instrumentation* (pp. 213–249). Hershey, PA: IGI Global. doi:10.4018/978-1-5225-0299-9.ch009

Perez, H., Hernandez, B., Rudomin, I., & Ayguade, E. (2016). Task-Based Crowd Simulation for Heterogeneous Architectures. In Q. Hassan (Ed.), *Innovative Research and Applications in Next-Generation High Performance Computing* (pp. 194–219). Hershey, PA: IGI Global. doi:10.4018/978-1-5225-0287-6.ch008

Pourqasem, J., & Edalatpanah, S. (2016). Verification of Super-Peer Model for Query Processing in Peer-to-Peer Networks. In Q. Hassan (Ed.), *Innovative Research and Applications in Next-Generation High Performance Computing* (pp. 306–332). Hershey, PA: IGI Global. doi:10.4018/978-1-5225-0287-6. ch012

Pujari, M., & Kanawati, R. (2016). Link Prediction in Complex Networks. In N. Meghanathan (Ed.), *Advanced Methods for Complex Network Analysis* (pp. 58–97). Hershey, PA: IGI Global. doi:10.4018/978-1-4666-9964-9.ch003

Qian, H., Yong, W., Jia, L., & Mengfei, C. (2016). Publish/Subscribe and JXTA based Cloud Service Management with QoS. *International Journal of Grid and High Performance Computing*, 8(3), 24–37. doi:10.4018/IJGHPC.2016070102

Raigoza, J., & Karande, V. (2017). A Study and Implementation of a Movie Recommendation System in a Cloud-based Environment. *International Journal of Grid and High Performance Computing*, 9(1), 25–36. doi:10.4018/IJGHPC.2017010103

Ramalingam, V. V. S., M., Sugumaran, V., V., V., & Vadhanam, B. R. (2017). Controlling Prosthetic Limb Movements Using EEG Signals. In M. S., & V. V. (Eds.), Multi-Core Computer Vision and Image Processing for Intelligent Applications (pp. 211-233). Hershey, PA: IGI Global. doi:10.4018/978-1-5225-0889-2.ch008

Rawat, D. B., & Bhattacharya, S. (2016). Wireless Body Area Network for Healthcare Applications. In N. Meghanathan (Ed.), *Advanced Methods for Complex Network Analysis* (pp. 343–358). Hershey, PA: IGI Global. doi:10.4018/978-1-4666-9964-9.ch014

Rehman, M. H., Khan, A. U., & Batool, A. (2016). Big Data Analytics in Mobile and Cloud Computing Environments. In Q. Hassan (Ed.), *Innovative Research and Applications in Next-Generation High Performance Computing* (pp. 349–367). Hershey, PA: IGI Global. doi:10.4018/978-1-5225-0287-6. ch014

Rico-Diaz, A. J., Rodriguez, A., Puertas, J., & Bermudez, M. (2017). Fish Monitoring, Sizing, and Detection Using Stereovision, Laser Technology, and Computer Vision. In M. S., & V. V. (Eds.), Multi-Core Computer Vision and Image Processing for Intelligent Applications (pp. 190-210). Hershey, PA: IGI Global. doi:10.4018/978-1-5225-0889-2.ch007

Rodriguez, A., Rico-Diaz, A. J., Rabuñal, J. R., & Gestal, M. (2017). Fish Tracking with Computer Vision Techniques: An Application to Vertical Slot Fishways. In M. S., & V. V. (Eds.), Multi-Core Computer Vision and Image Processing for Intelligent Applications (pp. 74-104). Hershey, PA: IGI Global. doi:10.4018/978-1-5225-0889-2.ch003

S., J. R., & Omman, B. (2017). A Technical Assessment on License Plate Detection System. In M. S., & V. V. (Eds.), *Multi-Core Computer Vision and Image Processing for Intelligent Applications* (pp. 234-258). Hershey, PA: IGI Global. doi:10.4018/978-1-5225-0889-2.ch009

Saadat, N., & Rahmani, A. M. (2016). A Two-Level Fuzzy Value-Based Replica Replacement Algorithm in Data Grids. *International Journal of Grid and High Performance Computing, 8*(4), 78–99. doi:10.4018/IJGHPC.2016100105

Sah, P., & Sarma, K. K. (2015). Bloodless Technique to Detect Diabetes using Soft Computational Tool. In K. Sarma, M. Sarma, & M. Sarma (Eds.), *Intelligent Applications for Heterogeneous System Modeling and Design* (pp. 139–158). Hershey, PA: IGI Global. doi:10.4018/978-1-4666-8493-5.ch006

Sahoo, B., Jena, S. K., & Mahapatra, S. (2014). Heuristic Resource Allocation Algorithms for Dynamic Load Balancing in Heterogeneous Distributed Computing System. In B. Tripathy & D. Acharjya (Eds.), *Advances in Secure Computing, Internet Services, and Applications* (pp. 181–209). Hershey, PA: IGI Global. doi:10.4018/978-1-4666-4940-8.ch010

Sarma, M., & Sarma, K. K. (2015). Acoustic Modeling of Speech Signal using Artificial Neural Network: A Review of Techniques and Current Trends. In K. Sarma, M. Sarma, & M. Sarma (Eds.), *Intelligent Applications for Heterogeneous System Modeling and Design* (pp. 282–299). Hershey, PA: IGI Global. doi:10.4018/978-1-4666-8493-5.ch012

Shahid, A., Arif, S., Qadri, M. Y., & Munawar, S. (2016). Power Optimization Using Clock Gating and Power Gating: A Review. In Q. Hassan (Ed.), *Innovative Research and Applications in Next-Generation High Performance Computing* (pp. 1–20). Hershey, PA: IGI Global. doi:10.4018/978-1-5225-0287-6.ch001

Shahid, A., Khalid, B., Qadri, M. Y., Qadri, N. N., & Ahmed, J. (2016). Design Space Exploration Using Cycle Accurate Simulator. In Q. Hassan (Ed.), *Innovative Research and Applications in Next-Generation High Performance Computing* (pp. 66–79). Hershey, PA: IGI Global. doi:10.4018/978-1-5225-0287-6.ch004

Shahid, A., Murad, M., Qadri, M. Y., Qadri, N. N., & Ahmed, J. (2016). Hardware Transactional Memories: A Survey. In Q. Hassan (Ed.), *Innovative Research and Applications in Next-Generation High Performance Computing* (pp. 47–65). Hershey, PA: IGI Global. doi:10.4018/978-1-5225-0287-6.ch003

Sharma, O., & Saini, H. (2017). SLA and Performance Efficient Heuristics for Virtual Machines Placement in Cloud Data Centers. *International Journal of Grid and High Performance Computing*, *9*(3), 17–33. doi:10.4018/IJGHPC.2017070102

Sheikh, A. (2017). Utilizing an Augmented Reality System to Address Phantom Limb Syndrome in a Cloud-Based Environment. *International Journal of Grid and High Performance Computing*, *9*(1), 14–24. doi:10.4018/IJGHPC.2017010102

Shojafar, M., Cordeschi, N., & Baccarelli, E. (2016). Resource Scheduling for Energy-Aware Reconfigurable Internet Data Centers. In Q. Hassan (Ed.), *Innovative Research and Applications in Next-Generation High Performance Computing* (pp. 21–46). Hershey, PA: IGI Global. doi:10.4018/978-1-5225-0287-6.ch002

Singh, S., & Gond, S. (2016). Green Computing and Its Impact. In G. Deka, G. Siddesh, K. Srinivasa, & L. Patnaik (Eds.), *Emerging Research Surrounding Power Consumption and Performance Issues in Utility Computing* (pp. 69–83). Hershey, PA: IGI Global. doi:10.4018/978-1-4666-8853-7.ch004

Sirisha, D., & Vijayakumari, G. (2017). Towards Efficient Bounds on Completion Time and Resource Provisioning for Scheduling Workflows on Heterogeneous Processing Systems. *International Journal of Grid and High Performance Computing*, *9*(3), 60–82. doi:10.4018/IJGHPC.2017070105

Sk, K., Mukherjee, M., & Maitra, M. (2017). FPGA-Based Re-Configurable Architecture for Window-Based Image Processing. In M. S., & V. V. (Eds.), Multi-Core Computer Vision and Image Processing for Intelligent Applications (pp. 1-46). Hershey, PA: IGI Global. doi:10.4018/978-1-5225-0889-2.ch001

Skanderova, L., & Zelinka, I. (2016). Differential Evolution Dynamic Analysis in the Form of Complex Networks. In N. Meghanathan (Ed.), *Advanced Methods for Complex Network Analysis* (pp. 285–318). Hershey, PA: IGI Global. doi:10.4018/978-1-4666-9964-9.ch012

Sreekumar, & Patel, G. (2014). Assessment of Technical Efficiency of Indian B-Schools: A Comparison between the Cross-Sectional and Time-Series Analysis. In B. Tripathy, & D. Acharjya (Eds.), *Advances in Secure Computing, Internet Services, and Applications* (pp. 128-139). Hershey, PA: IGI Global. doi:10.4018/978-1-4666-4940-8.ch007

Srinivasa, K. G., Hegde, G., Sideesh, G. M., & Hiriyannaiah, S. (2016). A Viability Analysis of an Economical Private Cloud Storage Solution Powered by Raspberry Pi in the NSA Era: A Survey and Analysis of Cost and Security. In G. Deka, G. Siddesh, K. Srinivasa, & L. Patnaik (Eds.), *Emerging Research Surrounding Power Consumption and Performance Issues in Utility Computing* (pp. 220–232). Hershey, PA: IGI Global. doi:10.4018/978-1-4666-8853-7. ch010

Srinivasa, K. G., Siddesh, G. M., Hiriyannaiah, S., Mishra, K., Prajeeth, C. S., & Talha, A. M. (2016). GPU Implementation of Friend Recommendation System using CUDA for Social Networking Services. In G. Deka, G. Siddesh, K. Srinivasa, & L. Patnaik (Eds.), *Emerging Research Surrounding Power Consumption and Performance Issues in Utility Computing* (pp. 304–319). Hershey, PA: IGI Global. doi:10.4018/978-1-4666-8853-7.ch015

Swargiary, D., Paul, J., Amin, R., & Bordoloi, H. (2015). Eye Ball Detection Using Labview and Application for Design of Obstacle Detector. In K. Sarma, M. Sarma, & M. Sarma (Eds.), *Intelligent Applications for Heterogeneous System Modeling and Design* (pp. 186–203). Hershey, PA: IGI Global. doi:10.4018/978-1-4666-8493-5.ch008

Swarnkar, M., & Bhadoria, R. S. (2016). Security Aspects in Utility Computing. In G. Deka, G. Siddesh, K. Srinivasa, & L. Patnaik (Eds.), *Emerging Research Surrounding Power Consumption and Performance Issues in Utility Computing* (pp. 262–275). Hershey, PA: IGI Global. doi:10.4018/978-1-4666-8853-7. ch012

Tchendji, V. K., Myoupo, J. F., & Dequen, G. (2016). High Performance CGM-based Parallel Algorithms for the Optimal Binary Search Tree Problem. *International Journal of Grid and High Performance Computing, 8*(4), 55–77. doi:10.4018/IJGHPC.2016100104

Tian, J., & Zhang, H. (2016). A Credible Cloud Service Model based on Behavior Graphs and Tripartite Decision-Making Mechanism. *International Journal of Grid and High Performance Computing, 8*(3), 38–56. doi:10.4018/IJGHPC.2016070103

Tiru, B. (2015). Exploiting Power Line for Communication Purpose: Features and Prospects of Power Line Communication. In K. Sarma, M. Sarma, & M. Sarma (Eds.), *Intelligent Applications for Heterogeneous System Modeling and Design* (pp. 320–334). Hershey, PA: IGI Global. doi:10.4018/978-1-4666-8493-5.ch014

Tripathy, B. K. (2014). Multi-Granular Computing through Rough Sets. In B. Tripathy & D. Acharjya (Eds.), *Advances in Secure Computing, Internet Services, and Applications* (pp. 1–34). Hershey, PA: IGI Global. doi:10.4018/978-1-4666-4940-8.ch001

Vadhanam, B. R. S., M., Sugumaran, V., V., V., & Ramalingam, V. V. (2017). Computer Vision Based Classification on Commercial Videos. In M. S., & V. V. (Eds.), Multi-Core Computer Vision and Image Processing for Intelligent Applications (pp. 105-135). Hershey, PA: IGI Global. doi:10.4018/978-1-5225-0889-2.ch004

Valero-Lara, P., Paz-Gallardo, A., Foster, E. L., Prieto-Matías, M., Pinelli, A., & Jansson, J. (2016). Multicore and Manycore: Hybrid Computing Architectures and Applications. In Q. Hassan (Ed.), *Innovative Research and Applications in Next-Generation High Performance Computing* (pp. 107–158). Hershey, PA: IGI Global. doi:10.4018/978-1-5225-0287-6.ch006

Winkler, M. (2016). Triadic Substructures in Complex Networks. In N. Meghanathan (Ed.), *Advanced Methods for Complex Network Analysis* (pp. 125–147). Hershey, PA: IGI Global. doi:10.4018/978-1-4666-9964-9.ch005

Xu, H., Rong, H., Mao, R., Chen, G., & Shan, Z. (2016). Hilbert Index-based Outlier Detection Algorithm in Metric Space. *International Journal of Grid and High Performance Computing, 8*(4), 34–54. doi:10.4018/IJGHPC.2016100103

Xu, R., & Faragó, A. (2016). Connectivity and Structure in Large Networks. In N. Meghanathan (Ed.), *Advanced Methods for Complex Network Analysis* (pp. 180–195). Hershey, PA: IGI Global. doi:10.4018/978-1-4666-9964-9.ch007

Youssef, B., Midkiff, S. F., & Rizk, M. R. (2016). SNAM: A Heterogeneous Complex Networks Generation Model. In N. Meghanathan (Ed.), *Advanced Methods for Complex Network Analysis* (pp. 215–236). Hershey, PA: IGI Global. doi:10.4018/978-1-4666-9964-9.ch009

Zahera, H. M., & El-Sisi, A. B. (2017). Accelerating Training Process in Logistic Regression Model using OpenCL Framework. *International Journal of Grid and High Performance Computing*, 9(3), 34–45. doi:10.4018/ IJGHPC.2017070103

Zelinka, I. (2016). On Mutual Relations amongst Evolutionary Algorithm Dynamics and Its Hidden Complex Network Structures: An Overview and Recent Advances. In N. Meghanathan (Ed.), *Advanced Methods for Complex Network Analysis* (pp. 319–342). Hershey, PA: IGI Global. doi:10.4018/978-1-4666-9964-9.ch013

Ziesche, S., & Yampolskiy, R. V. (2017). High Performance Computing of Possible Minds. *International Journal of Grid and High Performance Computing*, 9(1), 37–47. doi:10.4018/IJGHPC.2017010104

# About the Author

**B. K. Tripathy** is now working as a Senior Professor in SCOPE, VIT University, Vellore, India. He has received research/academic fellowships from UGC, DST, SERC and DOE of Govt. of India. Dr. Tripathy has published more than 480 technical papers in international journals, proceedings of international conferences and edited research volumes. He has produced 27 PhDs, 13 MPhils and 4 M.S (By research) under his supervision. He has published two text books on Soft Computing and Computer Graphics. Dr. Tripathy has served as the member of Advisory board or Technical Programme Committee member of several International conferences inside India and abroad. Also, he has edited four research volumes for IGI publications. He is a life/senior member of IEEE, ACM, IRSS, CSI, ACEEE, OMS, Indian Science Congress and IMS. Dr. Tripathy is an editorial board member/reviewer of more than 72 journals. His research interest includes Fuzzy Sets and Systems, Rough Sets and Knowledge Engineering, Data Clustering, Social Network Analysis, Soft Computing, Granular Computing, Content Based Learning, Neighbourhood Systems, Soft Set Theory, Social Internet of Things, Big Data Analytics, Theory of Multisets and List theory.

# Index

# R

Random perturbation 86-87
recursive 48, 86, 104-106, 111, 113-114
Reduced Model 133, 135
relational data 24, 30, 32, 36, 51

# S

sequential clustering 56-58
Social Network Anonymization 23, 36, 56
Social Network Anonymization Techniques 36
Social Network Representation 3
Social Network Security 16
Social Networks 1, 3-4, 6, 14, 16-17, 19, 21, 23-26, 34, 36, 49, 51, 58, 62, 68, 76, 78, 98, 107, 116-117, 120, 125, 135, 137-140, 144-146

structure 1-3, 26, 30, 43, 49, 69, 71, 86, 121, 140, 143, 145

# V

Vertex Clustering Methods 28, 52
Vertex-attribute Mapping Clustering methods 30, 52
vertices 4-8, 10, 13-14, 24-25, 29-32, 38, 41, 48, 51-56, 58-59, 61-64, 69, 71, 78-80, 86-88, 90, 93-99, 109, 116-117, 121-127
$\alpha$-anonymization 86, 107

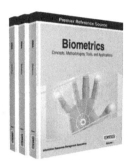

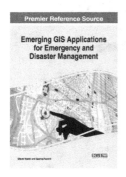   

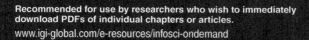